THE GOVERNMENT INSPECTOR

THE DRAMA LIBRARY

General Editor: EDWARD THOMPSON

THE GOVERNMENT INSPECTOR

by

NIKOLAI V. GOGOL

Translated and adapted by
D. J. CAMPBELL

Introduction by
JANKO LAVRIN

HEINEMANN
LONDON

Heinemann Educational Books Ltd
LONDON EDINBURGH MELBOURNE TORONTO AUCKLAND
KUALA LUMPUR SINGAPORE HONG KONG
NAIROBI JOHANNESBURG IBADAN
NEW DELHI

The Publishers of this edition would like to acknowledge their
grateful thanks to Messrs. The Sylvan Press Ltd. for permission
to reproduce the text of the play, together with the Foreword by
the translator, and the Introduction by Professor Janko Lavrin.

ISBN 0 435 20350 9

FIRST PUBLISHED BY THE SYLVAN PRESS 1947
FIRST PUBLISHED IN THE DRAMA LIBRARY 1953
REPRINTED, 1955, 1957, 1959, 1961, 1963, 1964,
1965, 1966, 1967 (twice), 1969 (twice), 1972 (twice)

PUBLISHED BY
HEINEMANN EDUCATIONAL BOOKS LTD
48 CHARLES STREET, LONDON WIX 8AH
PRINTED IN GREAT BRITAIN FOR THE PUBLISHERS BY
BUTLER AND TANNER LTD, FROME AND LONDON

CONTENTS

The play takes place during two days, about a century ago, in a town in Southern Russia.

CHARACTERS

ANTON ANTONOVITCH SKVOZNIK-DMUHANOVSKY	The Mayor
ANNA ANDREYEVNA	His Wife
MARYA ANTONOVNA	His daughter
LUKA LUKITCH HLOPOV	School Superintendent
HIS WIFE	
AMMOS FYODOROVITCH LYAPKIN-TYAPKIN	District Judge
ARTEMY FILIPOVITCH ZEMLYANIKA	Charity Commissioner
IVAN KOOSMITCH SHPYOKIN	Postmaster
PETER IVANOVITCH DOBCHINSKY	Town Landowner
PETER IVANOVITCH BOBCHINSKY	Town Landowner
IVAN ALEXANDROVITCH HLESTAKOV	A Junior Official from Petersburg
YOSIF	His servant
STEPAN ILYITCH UHOVYORTOV	Police Superintendent
IVAN LAZAREVITCH RASTAKOVSKY STEPAN IVANOVITCH KOROBKIN	Retired officials, men of consequence in the town
HIS WIFE	
SVISTOONOV DYERZHIMORDA	Constables
ABDULIN	A Merchant
SECOND MERCHANT	
THIRD MERCHANT	
MISHKA	A Servant
SERGEANT'S WIFE	
LOCKSMITH'S WIFE	
A WAITER IN THE INN	
A GENDARME	

*The following characters can be doubled :

YOSIF or MISHKA	can double	KOROBKIN
THE TWO CONSTABLES	,, ,,	SECOND & THIRD MERCHANTS
THE WAITER	,, ,,	RASTAKOVSKY

* In the Translator's Foreword this note is referred to as Appendix II.

vi

THE SERGEANT'S WIFE	can double KOROBKIN'S WIFE
THE LOCKSMITH'S WIFE	,, ,, HLOPOV'S WIFE
THE POLICE SUPERINTENDENT	,, ,, ABDULIN

The male doubles can be facilitated by using beards, and, for the merchants, flowing robes. Only the lower classes wore beards at the period of the play.

THE PRONUNCIATION OF RUSSIAN NAMES

GOGOL usually gave to his characters ludicrous or revealing surnames, in the manner of Dickens. In this play, that of the Mayor is supremely untranslatable, but means, roughly, " an empty-headed rascal " (" skvozik " means a draught of air). A few of the others are :

THE JUDGE	" Greedy snapper "
THE CHARITY COMMISSIONER	" Strawberry "
THE SCHOOL SUPERINTENDENT	" Bustle-bothered "
HLESTAKOV	" Torrents of fine talk "
THE TWO CONSTABLES	" Whistle-hit " and
	" Catch-hold-of-his-dial "

Obviously it makes no difference if these names are altered where they do not readily slip off English tongues, so long as they sound Russian. Actually the alleged difficulty of pronouncing Russian names is more psychological than real, and there is not a word in the script of this play which cannot be pronounced easily after a little practice. Y, unless final, is pronounced as in " yet," never as in " dryad " ; A as in " are " ; O as in " or " ; H as ch in " loch " ; U as " oo " ; R is rolled.

Hlestakov's servant is in the original called Osip, the colloquial and " peasanty " form of Yosif. Since " Osip " is difficult for English people to pronounce correctly, the change has been deliberately made.

The Russian mode of address by Christian name and father's name is too characteristic to be dispensed with, and these names should not be altered.

vii

INTRODUCTION

GOGOL THE PLAYWRIGHT

by

JANKO LAVRIN

I

THE world reputation of Nikolai Vasilyevitch Gogol (1809-1852) rests primarily on two of his works—the novel *Dead Souls*, and the satirical comedy *The Inspector-General*, or *The Government Inspector*—both of which are landmarks in the literature of his native country. While one of them played an outstanding part in the development of Russian fiction, the other is important for the history of the modern Russian theatre and drama. These two works are moreover complementary in so far as both of them bring out to perfection one of the basic features of Russian realism (or of what passes for it), namely its pathos of indictment, often fostered by all sorts of disillusions, especially those of a romantic kind. The gap between Gogol's own romantic aspirations and the life he saw around was largely responsible for that rancour with which he chastised reality for being what it was. Anxious to justify this attitude, in and through his art, he endeavoured to show life in its mean, ungainly aspects, and to exaggerate these to the point of grotesque caricature, at which he could laugh with all the bitterness inherent in his loud and infectious laughter. This is why so many of his characters are lowered to that subhuman level on which his comic exaggerations amount, now and then, to a hauntingly symbolic verdict against life as a whole. His *Dead Souls*, for instance, is a masterpiece of such symbolic " realism." And if *The Government*

Inspector is simpler not only in structure, but also in its impact, the laughter which permeates it is hardly less cruel and lashing than that in *Dead Souls*. This comedy is also one of the liveliest pieces of the entire Russian repertory ; and as for its characters, they have served for over a century as tests of good acting.

As a matter of fact, Gogol himself was something of an actor by nature. Most of his characters are visualised and depicted in terms of a comic impersonator. When as a young man he arrived from his native Ukraine to Petersburg in search of a post, he actually wanted to become an actor but was rejected on account of his weak voice. For this very reason he may have been all the more drawn to the stage. Its fascination proved so strong indeed that almost immediately after the success of his racy first stories, *Evenings on a Farm near the Dikanka* (1831-2), Gogol began to tackle two comedies, *The Order of Vladimir* and *The Wooers*, neither of which he finished. The first was to be a satire on Russian officialdom, but as if discouraged by the prospective conflicts with the censorship, he abandoned the venture. All that is left of it are three highly amusing fragments—*The Servant's Room*, *A Lawsuit*, and just *A Fragment*—rewritten in their present form considerably later, some time between 1837 and 1846. The principal character of the comedy was to be a bureaucratic careerist bent on getting the Order of Vladimir, but frustrated in this ambition, he was to go mad and to imagine that he was himself the coveted order.

The theme had partly been made use of in Gogol's well-known story, *The Diary of a Madman*, in which the original idea of the hero is split up between the humble clerk Poprishchin (who ends in a lunatic asylum) and his exalted chief. Yet the temptation to satirise the bureaucracy on the stage, once awakened, was much too strong to be given up. The more so because the satirical comedies of manners were already an established tradition in Russia and could show such examples as *The Brigadier* and *The Minor* by Fonvizin, Kapnist's *Chicane*, and Griboyedov's *Woe from Wit*. So in 1834 Gogol started writing his *Government Inspector*, and less than two years later the comedy was the greatest theatrical event of the season.

II

ON setting out to write this work, Gogol had little or no hope of ever seeing it performed, but an unexpected windfall saved the situation : the poet Zhukovsky, who was tutor to the heir apparent, showed Gogol's MS. to Nicholas I. The Tsar read it and was so impressed, that, censors or no censors, he himself ordered that *The Government Inspector* should be produced at the Imperial Theatre. Its first performance duly took place on March 19th, 1836 in the presence of the Tsar, who had his fill of laughter and summed up his impressions in the laconic phrase, " Everyone has received his due, and I most of all."

He did not exaggerate. Times and circumstances considered, the comedy was a daring piece of work, and the kind of laughter emanating from it could hardly be pleasing to a censor's ear. The actual theme is supposed to have been suggested by Pushkin, who in his inimitable manner related to Gogol how in Nizhni Novgorod he had once been mistaken for a high official, arrived incognito from Petersburg. Some further elements were gleaned from Kvitka's comedy on a similar theme, *A Newcomer from the Capital* (1827). Corneille's *Le Menteur* contributed what it could to the shaping of one of the two principal characters, Hlestakov, while in structure Gogol followed the general tradition of Molière which, incidentally, was quite conspicuous in the dramatic literature of Russia. He also chose the remote provincial background in which, as in a crooked mirror, everything looks funnier and more distorted than in reality.

The entire play is based on mistaken identity and on the panic caused—for good reasons—among the officials, headed by the *gorodnichy* (a kind of police governor of the town), when a hint is dropped that the Inspector-General is coming incognito from St. Petersburg. Their panic is so great as to make them take a smartly-dressed windbag, Hlestakov, for the dreaded Nemesis. Hlestakov, who is on his way to his father's farm, has lost at cards his last penny and is practically starving at the local inn when he is approached by the *gorodnichy*, trembling with anxiety, to find out whether and how it would be possible to bribe him. The *gorodnichy's* mission is crowned, of course, with immediate success. The supposed incognito is bribed also by the other culprits. He is lionised, fêted, shown the institutions in the town and eventually even " betrothed " to the *gorodnichy's* daughter. Conscious of his triumph, the *gorodnichy* grows more insolent, more bullying and grabbing than ever before. Hlestakov departs " for a few days," his head full of alcohol and happy memories, and his pockets bulging with money. Proud of his exalted son-in-law, the *gorodnichy* dreams of his own greatness to come, when the identity-mistake is suddenly discovered, and at the height of general consternation a gendarme appears with the announcement that the Inspector-General has arrived and wants to see the *gorodnichy* without delay.

The plot thus offered great satirical possibilities which were exploited by the author to the full. Having skilfully combined the comicality of the situations with that of the characters, he knew how to combine equally well the cracking of his whip with his uproarious laughter. But a word should be said on behalf of Hlestakov, who is neither a scheming nor even a conscious liar, but just a nonentity seizing the first opportunity of displaying his imaginary importance. In this he finds a compensation for his actual insignificance, and so he is the first to believe in all he says, or pretends to be. He is in short one of the most consummate *innocent* liars in literature. Another virtue of the play consists in the compactness of its structure as well as in the swift pace of the action itself. This is what Belinsky, the leading critic of that period, said of it : " In *The Government Inspector* there are no scenes to which the word ' better ' can be applied, because none of them is superior to others. They are all indispensable parts of one artistic whole, rounded off by its form and its contents, and thus constituting a self-sufficient world of its own."

III

It goes without saying that but for the Tsar's intercession the play would not have seen the stage for quite a long time. But the very fact that it was produced had some interesting and even paradoxical consequences. Whereas the liberal-minded spectators were ready to see in such an event a kind of political and moral victory over the " leaden regime " of those years, those ridiculed in it were fuming with indignation and did all they could to suppress it. Gogol first turned against them in a dramatic post-script, *Homegoing After The Show*, in which he stressed the fact that the chief character in his play was really laughter in its salutary ethical function. Later he expressed a similar idea in his *An Author's Confession*, where he frankly acknowledged that only beginning with *The Government Inspector* had his own laughter acquired a moral *raison d'être*. " I saw that in my earlier works I laughed for nothing, uselessly, in vain, and without knowing why. But if one is to laugh, then let us at least laugh at those things which deserve to be laughed at."

That was precisely what he did in his comedy. But what he failed to anticipate was the hostility such a campaign was bound to arouse in a country where corruption was almost inseparable from the regime itself. So a hue and cry against the " unpatriotic " play continued. Gogol became so disgusted with it all that in the end he decided to leave Russia. He settled down in Rome where, but for two short visits to his native land, he spent most of his time between 1836 and 1848. It was during his stay abroad, too, that certain inner dilemmas, rather important for Gogol's further fate, came to a head.

It should be borne in mind that those were the years of mental fermentation in Russia herself, and that Gogol, even while abroad, could not but take part in it. With Pushkin's tragic death in 1837 the so-called gentry period of Russian culture came to an end and was being gradually replaced by the " intelligentsia " period which lasted until the revolution in 1917. The formative process of the intelligentsia (itself a somewhat classless compound of progressively-minded noblemen and educated commoners), continued well-nigh into the 'sixties, and the ideological battles, notably those fought between the Westerners and the Slavophils, were tough at times.

The death of Pushkin, which took place at the beginning of that process, left a cultural gap behind, and Gogol—the most significant talent after Pushkin—could not help feeling that the leadership in Russian literature had now fallen on his shoulders. Aware of the responsibility involved, he naturally looked upon such a task not only from an æsthetic but also from an ethical angle. In the completed first part of *Dead Souls* he actually balanced the two ; but in the few preserved chapters of the second part (the final MS. of which he burned in a fit of religious mania shortly before his death) the two are already divorced, and the moral or rather moralising " purpose " runs riot. So it does in *The Denouement of the Government Inspector* (1846), in which Gogol tried to interpret even that comedy in a highfalutin allegorical manner. The God-forsaken provincial hole, bullied by its *gorodnichy*, was suddenly declared to be the city of the soul ; Hlestakov was nothing less than its " worldly " conscience, whereas the Inspector at the end of the play became the " true " conscience which each of us will have to face after death.

All this is of course nonsense, yet as a symptom of Gogol's own moral crisis it may be of great interest. It was above all the powerful effect *The Government Inspector* had had upon the audiences that opened Gogol's eyes to the moral significance of laughter and consequently also to the responsibilities of a comic author of his stamp. The famous comedy thus had a considerable bearing on its author's inner life, the complications of which need not detain us in an Introduction of this size. A few words must be said, however, about Gogol's further dramatic activities.

IV

LIKE Griboyedov's *Woe from Wit*, and Pushkin's *Boris Godunov*, *The Government Inspector* was one of the outstanding major dramatic works in Russia during the first half of the nineteenth century. As has already been mentioned, Gogol made several other ventures in the realm of drama, but only *The Marriage* (1842), in which he developed certain elements of his one-time *Wooers*, has definitely conquered the stage. This work is nearer to farcical comedy than to a satire, but its characters, as well as its quick vivacious pace, bear the authentic stamp of Gogol. Its chief fun is provided by the meeting-ground between the " noble " officials in search of rich brides, and the old-fashioned merchants' *milieu*, where such brides were to be found. That was precisely the *milieu* which was taken up, partly in the footsteps of Gogol, by the greatest realistic playwright in Russian literature, Alexander Ostrovsky.

English readers may perhaps be interested in the fact that almost concurrently with *The Government Inspector* Gogol thought of writing a tragedy from English history, but the few jottings he left (under the title *Alfred*) will hardly make one regret that the play was never written. Quite a different matter is his one-act comedy *The Gamblers* (1842). Here we feel again Gogol's flair for the grotesque, for quickness of action, as well as for dramatic suspense. There are only male parts in this play on the theme of cheating the cheat, but this is all for the better, since Gogol was never quite successful in his portraits of women.

Such, on the whole, is a brief account of Gogol the playwright. In conclusion we should add that his dramatic work, notably *The Government Inspector*, contributed a great deal to the evolution of the peculiar Russian realism in acting—no doubt because at the very outset such a talented actor as Shchepkin set up a very high standard in the part of the *gorodnichy*. Shchepkin's realism was further developed by Sadovskoy in Ostrovsky's plays, but the climax of the character-study on the stage was reached, beyond doubt, in the Moscow Art Theatre, the repertory of which included from its earliest days *The Government Inspector*, and *The Marriage*. Both of them enjoy now an international reputation. No doubt they will continue to do so.

University College, Nottingham.

FOREWORD

THIS play is perhaps the greatest comedy ever written for the Russian stage, and is universally popular in the Soviet Union to-day. Written in 1834, during the reign of the martinet Tsar, Nicholas I, it would normally have stood no chance of passing the ignorant and illiberal censorship of the time, and like many another such work, would not have been seen in print or performance until the Revolution. But, as related by Prof. Lavrin in his Introduction, the poet Zhukovsky took the play to the Tsar, who was delighted with it, and ordered its production. His patronage helped to ward off for a time the attacks of the officialdom satirised by the play.

The Civil Service of Tsarist Russia was organised on a basis introduced by Peter the Great from Germany. It was classified into fourteen grades, or ranks, which were the equivalents of the commissioned ranks in the Army and Navy. A similar system embraced even the Church, and nearly everyone except petty traders and serfs was classified in this framework. The ranks in the Civil Service bore titles with no relation to the duties involved, and each rank had its uniform and title of address. The characters introduce themselves in Act III, Scene 1, by giving the name of the post held, rank, and surname. Thus, the Mayor is the equivalent of a colonel, the Charity Commissioner and Postmaster of a lieutenant-colonel, the Judge of a major, and the School Superintendent of a captain. Hlestakov is in the lowest grade, equivalent to the rank of cornet or ensign.

All officials were responsible to St. Petersburg. It may be

noted in passing that even the judicature was part of the civil service, and shared its viewpoints and vices.

NOTES FOR THE PRODUCER

The chief authority of a district town, such as that of the play, was a " *gorodnichy*," a police official primarily charged with maintaining order. " Prefect " would be a better translation of the Russian word, but I have followed most other translators in calling him the Mayor, as it is a more effective word.

Gogol's descriptions of his characters are as follows :

THE MAYOR. He has grown old in the service, and in his own opinion is far from being a fool. He has taken bribes for many years, but he bears himself with the dignity of a conscientious public servant. He is serious, even a little sententious ; he is neither talkative nor taciturn, and his voice is neither loud nor soft. His every word is significant. The lines of his face are hard and rough, as is usual with men who have gone through hard times in the lower ranks. [It is the face of the " ranker officer." D.J.C.] His transitions from fear to rejoicing, from haughtiness to chastened humility, are rapid ; they are those of a man of coarsely developed, gross instincts.

He is generally dressed in his uniform with facings, and knee boots with spurs. His hair is dark, worn in a military cut or *en brosse*. It is speckled with grey.

ANNA ANDREYEVNA, his wife, is the provincial kind of coquette. She is in early middle-age. Her mind was formed partly by novelettes and scrap-books, partly by the bustle of household duties and the supervision of maidservants. She is very curious, and at times very vain. Sometimes she dominates her husband, simply because he is at a loss for a reply to her, but this dominance only occurs over trifling matters and consists of derision and reproving remarks. She changes her clothes four times during the play.

YOSIF, Hlestakov's servant, is like most elderly servants. His talk is rather slow and serious, he tends to keep his eyes on the floor. He is fond of repeating to himself moral maxims, intended to improve his master's character. His voice is level, but in conversation with his master takes on an abrupt, rough, and even harsh tone. He is cleverer than his master, because he is " quicker in the uptake." He is a rascal, but rather a taciturn rascal. He wears a grey or blue coat, not overly clean or new.

BOBCHINSKY and DOBCHINSKY are both little men, scatter-brained, and inordinately curious. They are very much alike, both middle-aged, and with slight *en bon point*. They speak quickly and volubly with much gesticulation. Dobchinsky is a little the taller and more serious of the two, Bobchinsky more lively and free-and-easy.

LYAPKIN-TYAPKIN, THE JUDGE, is a man who has read five or six books in his life, and is in consequence a free-thinker. He is a great spinner of theories, and gives his words great weight. The man who plays this part must never allow his face to lose the look of a man who ponders weighty matters. He speaks in a deep bass voice, rather hoarse and cracked, which reminds one of an old-fashioned clock that wheezes before it strikes.

ZEMLYANIKA, THE CHARITY COMMISSIONER, is a fat man, disproportionate and clumsy, but a rogue and intriguer. He is bustling and officious.

SHPYOKIN, THE POSTMASTER, is simple-hearted to the point of naïveté.

The other parts do not need any special explanations, with the exception of

HLESTAKOV, the leading rôle. He is a slim, almost skinny young man of 23. He is rather silly and scatter-brained ; what is called shallow. He talks and acts without any reflection. He is incapable of sustained attention to any-thing. His speech is staccato, and the words come out of his mouth quite unpredictably. The more the actor of this part displays frankness, ingenuousness, and simplicity, the more successful it is. He is dressed in the fashion of the period.

After the first production, which Gogol felt to have been a

failure, although it was an instant popular success, he dwelt in letters to friends on the play as a whole, and especially on the character of Hlestakov, the creation of which by the actor Dur, he felt to have been a travesty of his intentions.

" The leading rôle was a failure; I had expected this. Dur showed not the smallest comprehension of the character of Hlestakov. He made him a common humbug . . . the familiar scapegrace of Paris vaudeville. . . .

" Hlestakov is not a professional fraud or a deliberate impostor. He forgets that he is lying and almost believes his own words. He unfolds himself; as his spirits rise he soars into flights of fancy. Seeing that everything goes well, that people hang on his words, he speaks more fluently, more freely; he unfolds his inmost desires with complete frankness and in doing so, displays himself as he is.

" Hlestakov does not lie coldly and deliberately, but theatrically and passionately. His eyes light up. It is the best and most inspired moment of his life. . . .

" In Hlestakov nothing must be harsh or stiff. . . .

" Occasionally he behaves or speaks with sense. It is when character and mind are required that his foolish, insignificant nature is revealed. . . .

" Analyse Hlestakov and what is he? A young man, an official, shallow, but containing many traits common to people that the world does not consider shallow. Displaying these traits, or particular failings, in people who are not devoid of good qualities, would be an offence from the author's standpoint, because it would hold them up to general ridicule. Better to let everyone discover a fragment of himself in this rôle, and at the same time look round without having to fear the pointed finger of scorn. In a word, Hlestakov is the type of much that is scattered through various Russian characters, and which is here fortuitously united in one. Every one of us is, or has been, Hlestakov, but, naturally, we do not like to admit it. We mock at him inside other men's skins, but not in our own. . . .

" I thought that one day an actor of many-sided talents would be grateful to me for uniting in one character such diverse motifs, and giving him the opportunity to display simultaneously the manifold facets of his art."

"The other leading rôle of the play is that of the Mayor, whose chief concern is lest he lose anything ' that swims into his hands.' Because of this concern he has no time to examine himself or to take a critical view of life. Because of this concern, and possibly without realising it, he has become a tyrant, but this is not due to any innate malice or urge to tyranny. He is inspired only by the desire to grab whatever he sets eyes on. He has rather forgotten that in doing so he sets his foot on his neighbour's neck. But at times he does feel his guilt, and then he prays, goes to church, and tells himself that he is at least firm in the faith. Sometimes he even ponders the idea of confessing everything and doing penance. But the lure of worldly possessions, the thought of all the things he might acquire and the dread of missing anything have become with him habits too deeply rooted ever to be overcome.

"He has been staggered by the spreading report about an Inspector-General, and still more by the fact that this Inspector will arrive incognito, at a time and by means unknown. During the whole of the play he is jolted out of his normal existence ; his face is haggard, his eyes bloodshot and burning.

"When the Inspector does come, proving less terrible than he expected, and even wants to marry his daughter, he puffs himself up with such ridiculous dreams of greatness that when the bubble does burst it falls on him as a thunder-clap ; the shock is far worse for him than for the others, and his position is truly a tragic one."

The play is notable for its large number of small parts. I have cut three that serve no purpose in an English version and framed the rest to render doubling easy. (A list of feasible doubles is given in Appendix II.) Generally I have changed the original arrangement and dialogue as little as possible, and the five scenes of this version correspond generally to the five acts of the original. Gogol's scanty stage directions have been amplified to the degree now usual.

The way in which this play opens, the immediate plunge *in medias res*, is masterly and has been rightly praised ; but for non-Russian audiences, who cannot be expected to know the state of local government in Russia in the 1830's, the first ten minutes or so are very confusing. I believe that this, with the largeness of the caste, are the chief reasons why this play has never attained in Britain the popularity which is its due.

The only remedy is the insertion, before the Mayor's entrance, of a short scene introducing the officials, the milieu and the atmosphere, but such an insertion is very undesirable in a published adaptation. I did, in all humility, write such a scene when this version was first produced (by Mr. Nugent Monck, at the Maddermarket Theatre, Norwich); copies are available if any producer wishes to consider this expedient. The scene plays two-and-a-half minutes.

Hlestakov's soliloquies are essential but I have made him speak one to Yosif. I have ended Act II Sc. 2 with his exit and grafted the remainder of Gogol's Act III into the following act, which he observed to open a little weakly. The third act of this version is a little too long, but of the three possible ways in which Gogol's five acts can be arranged in three, that adopted is held to give the best division of interest.

Gogol was dissatisfied with the original production and rewrote about half the play. I have used his revisions where they seem to me to be improvements, but in most cases his first thoughts were best.

The Russian play contains numerous asides, some containing important comedy points, others valuable for character indications. After much thought I have decided to retain the best of these, with the idea in mind, that the producer will consider each individual case with the actor, and decide whether the line is to be treated as written, rendered by gesture or facial expression, or spoken to another actor. The Mayor's asides in the inn scene are the most important, and should receive special care.

It may be necessary to emphasise that this play is not a farce, neither are the characters intended to be mere caricatures of the wretched officialdom of the period. They are human people, chips of the " Russian soul " ; their weaknesses, thievings, lyings, mental contortions, self-justifications, browbeatings, betrayals, briberies and braggadocio are entirely representative and consistent. They are fine studies in the degradation of the human mind, forged at white heat in the scorn of a man who had explored the frailties of humanity. The satire comes from faithfully reproducing them on the stage for what they are. To dehumanise such characters is to admit failure to see humanity in the round. In Gogol's words :

" The main thing to guard against is caricature. There must be nothing exaggerated or trivial even in the characters of low social class, e.g., the petitioners in Act III. . . . The less the actor thinks about being funny, the funnier his rôle will be. The humour will be measured by the seriousness, the absorption in his own affairs, which each character shows in his face. Each of them is anxiously, bustlingly, even ardently bound up in his own affairs, as if they were the most important thing in life. Only the spectator sees how trifling are their anxieties. But the characters themselves never joke, and indeed they never dream that anyone might be laughing at them. The experienced actor, before he gets hold of the more delicate oddities, and the finer external peculiarities of the part submitted to him, must strive to attain its fundamental human expression ; he must find out why the part has been invoked, what the principal and pre-eminent concern of the character is, to which his or her life is devoted, and which forms the constant subject of thought."

Some critics have found an element of caricature in the play, and some producers have emphasised this caricature, or selective distortion, with the aid of stage devices, but the play has then ceased to be the one Gogol wrote. He never admitted his play to be a caricature or a farce, though he stated that it is far easier to play the parts as caricatures than to lay hold of the true character lines.

On the other hand, there is obviously condensation and exaggeration of the evils of bureaucracy without democracy (critics of the first production protested that there was not such a town in all Russia), but these features are common to all satire, and Gogol expressly admits them.

Since 1917 the view has been put forward that the play has lost its meaning, and that there is no point in satirising a class which has been swept away. But this view is short-sighted ; it would sweep into the discard not only *The Government Inspector* but much of Ibsen, much of Shaw, and hundreds of the world's store of masterpieces. In this play the direct object of satire is the

Tsarist bureaucracy, but the indirect object is a range of attitudes of mind, and patterns of behaviour which were not confined to that bureaucracy, but which are widespread in the world to-day. The unscrupulous business man " on the make," the mischief- and intrigue-maker, and other character types all have their analogues in the play, and Gogol's remark that everyone will find something of himself in Hlestakov, is to some extent true of the other characters. Gogol was really ridiculing a much wider field of rottenness than the officialdom he knew, and said so in his last comment on the play, written near the end of his life :

" In *The Government Inspector* I tried to gather in one heap all that was bad in Russia. I wished to turn it all into ridicule. The real impression produced was that of fear. Through the laughter that I have never laughed more loudly, the spectator feels my bitterness and sorrow."

*   *   *   *   *

I am indebted to Sykes' translation (1892) for some of the background information mentioned in this Foreword, and for the text of the last paragraph, the original of which I have not been able to find. It is a pleasure to acknowledge Prof. Lavrin's valuable advice, and the Rev. W. H. Marshall's kindness in reading the proofs. Responsibility for the text is, of course, solely mine.

D. J. CAMPBELL

Grantham 1946

ACT I

*A room in the Mayor's house; the furnishings are approximately
Empire, very varied, and reveal some lack of taste; up centre are folding
doors, the usual entry; up right a door leading to a bedroom, and right a
window, which is practical; up left is a door leading to the rest of the
house; there is no open fireplace, but a Russian stove on the wall, left;
this looks like a large cabinet or wardrobe, without legs, and warms the
room by the heat from its walls; it is painted to represent enamel and is
in use, as it is winter; there is a chandelier and also candelabra here and
there, but these are only illuminated in Act I and Act III, Sc. 1; there
is a sofa, a table, and numerous chairs. It is morning, about 8 o'clock. At
curtain rise the Judge, the Charity Commissioner, and the School Superintendent are discovered, in various attitudes of waiting; they should con-
vey a feeling of uneasy anticipation; the Judge is sprawling in a chair and
for him and Hlopov this is clearly " the morning after "; he strives to
focus on his watch but cannot manage it; Hlopov paces nervously; his
dress has been rather hastily put on; the Charity Commissioner stands by
the window with a more confident air, but even he, like the others, glances
uneasily now and then at the door, left. Enter the Mayor; he is in uniform; the Judge rises at once and all three pay respectful attention.*

MAYOR : (*briskly*) Good morning, gentlemen. I asked you here
this morning because I have some very unpleasant news for
you. I have found out that an Inspector-General is coming
from Petersburg with secret orders to inspect our province,
and especially everything to do with our district. He will
travel incognito.

JUDGE : What are you saying ? From Petersburg ?

CC. : With secret orders ?

SS. : And incognito !

MAYOR : I don't like the business any better than you do. But,
you know, I had a premonition of it. I was dreaming all last
night about two enormous rats ! Upon my soul, I never saw
such brutes, huge black ones ! They came, sniffed, and went
away again ! But I'll read you the letter I've just had from
Tchmíhov ; (*to CC.*) You know him, Artémy Filípovitch. He
writes : " Dear friend, godfather, and benefactor " (*he
mutters under his breath, eyes moving swiftly.*) Ah ! This is it :
". . . and I hasten to warn you that an official is coming to

23

inspect the whole province, and especially our district. I have learned this from an absolutely trustworthy source, although the man passes himself off as a private person. I know you are like all the rest of us and have your little failings, for being a sensible fellow you don't like to lose what swims into your hands." (*disconcerted, but looks up saying:*) Oh well, we're all friends here. " I warn you to take precautions, as he may arrive any moment, if he hasn't already arrived and is living somewhere incognito. The other day I . . ." The rest is only about family matters, " my cousin A'nna Kirílovna and her husband are staying with us. He has got very stout and is always playing the fiddle," and so on, and so on. Well, there you are, gentlemen.

JUDGE : But it's extraordinary, simply extraordinary !

SS. : Tell me please, Antón Antónovitch, why this has happened. Why send an Inspector to us ? Our town is so far away. Why should they care about us ?

MAYOR : Why ? It must be fate. Up to now, God has been good to us, they've pried into other towns ; we never had anything like this. Well now, it's our turn.

JUDGE : I believe, Anton Antonovitch, there's some deep, far-reaching political reason for this. I have it ! Russia is going to war, and the Ministry has sent this man to find out . . . Yes ! To find out if there is treason anywhere !

MAYOR : What next ? And you an intelligent man ! Treason in a country town ! Is this the frontier ? You could gallop from here for three years and not reach a foreign country !

JUDGE : No, you're wrong. Petersburg may be far away, but the authorities don't miss much. They see everything !

MAYOR : (*uneasily*) Well, they may, or they may not. That doesn't matter now. This Inspector may even now be undoing us all behind our own backs. As to my own special responsibilities, the police, and the general good order of the town, I have already taken some steps, and I advise you to do the same. (*swinging round on CC.*) Especially you, Artemy Filipovitch ; this official will certainly inspect your institutions, and you had better see they look decent ! Get some clean nightcaps and bedclothes, the ones you've got are enough for a report in themselves. And the patients might look a little less like chimney sweeps !

CC. : That's nothing much. I may be able to find some clean nightcaps.

MAYOR : And there ought to be some way of distinguishing the patients. Put a sign over each bed, and get the doctor to put up, in Latin or some such language, the names of the patients when admitted, their diseases, and so on. And make them stop smoking that filthy tobacco for a while, it makes me choke whenever I go in ! And get rid of some of the patients ; there are far too many. He'll think the doctor doesn't know his business !

CC. : Oh ! The doctor and I have got things well arranged in the medical line. The more natural your treatment is, the better. We don't bother with expensive medicines ! These patients are very simple people ! If they die, well ! they die ! If they get better, they get better ! And it would really be very difficult for Hiebner to talk to them. He's a very good doctor, but he doesn't know a word of Russian !

MAYOR : (*to Judge*) And you ought to do something about the state of your courthouse, A'mmos Fyódorovitch ! Your porter keeps geese in the anterooms, and goslings, and they run about and peck under your feet. Of course it's a good thing to keep poultry, very praiseworthy, but can't he keep them somewhere else ? It makes the place smell so !

JUDGE : That's a small matter. I can have them killed today. Would you like to come to dinner to-night ?

MAYOR : Then your offices are full of all kinds of rubbish. Skins hanging up to dry, and whips and gear mixed up with the papers. I know you're very fond of hunting, but why not tidy it up till this inspector's been, then you can put it all back, if you want to ! Then that clerk of yours ! He may know a great deal, but he gives off a powerful odour of vodka ! I've wanted to talk these things over with you for some time, but something has always turned up to put it out of my mind. If it really is his natural smell, as he says it is, there must be a remedy. Tell him to try eating onions, or perhaps the doctor could give him something or other.

JUDGE : No, it's no good. He says when he was a child his nurse bruised him, and he's given off a slight smell of vodka ever since.

MAYOR : Well, I thought I'd mention it. About your conduct in Court, and what Tchmihov in his letter calls " little failings " well ! What is there to say ? No man is without sin. It's God's will, and it is no use the free-thinkers arguing about it.

JUDGE : Well, there are sins and sins. I freely admit I take bribes, but what sort of bribes ? Borzoi puppies, that's all !

MAYOR : Whether it's Borzoi puppies or something else, it's still bribery.

JUDGE : But you're wrong there. For example, if a man takes a fur coat, worth 500 roubles, or a shawl for his wife . . .

MAYOR : (*who doesn't relish this line*) Well, what of it ? Only taking puppies as bribes won't save you. Why, you don't believe in God ! You never go to church ! As for me, I do at least believe devoutly, and I go to church every Sunday. But you . . . when you start talking about the creation of the world, it makes my hair stand on end !

JUDGE : Well, at least my opinions are my own. A man who thinks for himself. . . .

MAYOR : Sometimes much thinking is worse than none at all. As for the rest, I only mentioned about the district courthouse, but to tell the truth, hardly anyone is likely to look into it. It's in such a state, it must be under divine protection. (*wheeling round*) Now then, Luká Lúkitch, as the school superintendent it's your business to superintend the teachers. I know they're very learned men, educated in all kinds of colleges, but their behaviour is most peculiar. Perhaps that's the natural way of educated men, I don't know. There's one who's always making grimaces. He might put this Inspector in a very bad mood.

SS. : What can I do ? I did speak to him about it once ; it was the day the prince inspected us. That man pulled such a fearful face, I never saw anything like it ! I got a telling-off for letting the boys be taught wild, godless ideas !

MAYOR : Yes, yes. Now take the history teacher. He's an able chap, knows his subject, but he expounds it with so much heat, that there's no understanding him. I listened to him once ; while he was talking about the Assyrians and Babylonians, he was all right, but when he came to Alexander the Great, it was simply indescribable ! I thought the place was on fire ! He jumped down from his desk, took a chair and banged it on the floor, brandished it over his head ! I think he was describing a battle. Now Alexander the Great was a great general and all that, but why break the chairs, they're Government property ?

ss. : Yes, he's a hothead. I've spoken to him about it, but he just says, " As you wish, but I would lay down my life in the cause of learning ! "

MAYOR : Yes, it's a mysterious law of life. Clever men are never quite sane. They either drink, or go mad and make faces that would shock the saints !

ss. : Heaven help any man in the education line ! These clever fellows put me in a sweat whenever they open their mouths ! Always showing off !

MAYOR : It wouldn't matter but . . . it's this cursed incognito ! He may look in any minute and say, " Aha, My pets ! Here you are ! And who is Health Commissioner here ? Zemlyaníka. Hand over Zemlyanika ! And who is the judge ? Lyápkin-Tyápkin. Hand over Lyapkin-Tyapkin." It's awful !

[the door opens ; all jump; the Postmaster comes in.]

POSTM. : Tell me ; what's this about an Inspector, gentlemen ?

MAYOR : Have you only just heard ?

POSTM. : I heard something from Peter Ivánovitch Bóbchinsky. He's just been to see me at the post office.

MAYOR : What's your opinion ?

POSTM. : I think it means war with the Turks.

JUDGE : Just what I said ! My very words !

POSTM. : Yes ! It's all the fault of those filthy French !

MAYOR : (*great scorn*) War with the Turks ! You fool ! War with us, more likely ! We're the ones who are going to catch it, not the Turks ! This letter says that much !

POSTM. : Oh ! That's different. Maybe it won't be war with the Turks.

MAYOR : How do you feel about it, Iván Kóosmitch ?

POSTM. : Me ? Oh, I don't know. How do you feel ?

MAYOR : Well, I'm not frightened, but I am a little uneasy, about the trades-people. They say they've found me difficult, though God's my judge, if I have taken from one or two, I did it without any ill-feeling. (*links arms with PM. and takes him aside*) I even think there may have been some secret denunciation of me. Why else should they send an Inspector here ? Now listen, Ivan Koosmitch, this is for our mutual benefit. Couldn't you take every letter that passes through your post office, and, well, just unseal it a little bit, you know, and read it through. Then if there was no denunciation or anything, you could reseal it somehow, or send it on unsealed.

POSTM. : I know, I know. . . . You're not teaching me anything. I've done it for years, not just as a precaution ; I do like to know what goes on in the world. I tell you, it makes most interesting reading ! And so edifying !

MAYOR : Have you found anything about an official from Petersburg ?

POSTM. : No ! But plenty about those in Kostróma and Sarátov. It's a pity you did not read the letters. Wonderful tit-bits ! The other day a lieutenant wrote to a friend, describing a ball in most sprightly language, very, very nicely. " My life, dear friend, soars to Empyrean heights of pleasure," he wrote, " young women, music, hard riding." He described it with deep feeling. I kept it on purpose. Would you like to read it.

MAYOR : I can't be bothered now, but do me that favour, Ivan Kóosmitch. If you find any complaint or denunciation, don't stop to think, keep it back.

POSTM. : I'll do that with pleasure.

JUDGE : I warn you, you'll get into trouble some day for that.

MAYOR : Nonsense, nonsense. If you did anything publicly, mind, that would be different, but this is a family affair.

JUDGE : Yes, there'd soon be trouble. By the way, Anton Antonovitch, I was coming to show you my new bitch, own sister to the one you know about. Oh ! Have you heard about Cheptóvitch and Valínsky's lawsuit ? That's a great luxury to me. I'm in clover. I can go coursing one day on Cheptovitch's land, and the next on Valinsky's !

MAYOR : Holy Saints ! I'm not interested in your coursing just now ! It's this infernal incognito. . . . ! Having to sit here and wait till that door suddenly opens and . . .

[the door does suddenly open; all jump; enter Bobchinsky and Dobchinsky, panting.]

BOB. : Something extraordinary has happened !

DOB. : Most unexpected tidings !

ALL : What's happened ? What is it ?

DOB. : The strangest affair ! Quite unforeseen ! We were going into the inn . . .

BOB. : *(interrupting)* Yes, I was going into the inn with Peter Ivanovitch here *(indicates Dob.)*

DOB. : *(interrupting)* But let me tell it, Peter Ivanovitch !

BOB. : No ! Let me, let me . . . You haven't got the style . . . Permit me, p ease !

DOB. : But you'll get confused; you won't remember everything !

BOB. : No ! I shall remember ! So help me ! I shall remember it all ! Don't keep interfering. I'l tell it ! Tell him not to interfere !

MAYOR : Oh, for God's sake tell us what it's all about. My heart's in my mouth. Sit down everybody, find yourself seats. Here's a chair for you, Peter Ivanovitch. *(both Bob. and Dob. attempt to sit in it; all eager and attentive)*. Now then. What is it ?

BOB. : Allow me. I'll begin at the beginning and tell you everything. As soon as I had the pleasure of leaving you, after you received that letter, well then I was going along. *Please* don't interrupt, Peter Ivanovitch, I know *all* about it. Well, you must understand, I ran in to see Koróbkin, and as he wasn't at home I turned in to see Rastakóvsky, and as he wasn't at home I went to see Ivan Koosmitch here *(indicating Postmaster)* to communicate to him the news you had received, and leaving there I encountered Peter Ivanovitch *(indicating Dob.)*.

DOB. : Near the stall where they sell pies.

BOB. : Yes, near the stall where they sell pies. I met Peter Ivanovitch and I said, "Have you heard the news Anton Antonovitch has received in a letter?" Peter Ivanovitch had heard all about it from your housekeeper, Avdótya, who was sent for some reason to Pochéchuev's . . .

DOB. : To get a keg for the French brandy.

BOB. : (*in spite of himself*) To get a keg for French brandy. Please don't interrupt, don't interrupt. So we went to Pochechuev's and on the way he said to me, he said, "Let's go into the inn. My stomach . . . I've had nothing since morning, and it's rumbling so," that is, of course, Peter Ivanovitch's stomach. "Into the inn," he kept saying; "They have just got some fresh salmon in, and we could have just a snack." Well, we were in the inn, when a young man. . . .

DOB. : Of elegant appearance, but not in official uniform . . .

BOB. : Of elegant appearance, but not in official uniform . . ., came across the room, and his face had a kind of thoughtfulness, a—a—physiognomy, and a great deal, oh yes, a great deal, up here (*tapping forehead*). I had a kind of presentiment, and I said to Peter Ivanovitch, "There is more here than meets the eye." Yes. So we beckoned the innkeeper, you know, Vlass . . . his wife gave birth three weeks ago, and such an alert little fellow! He'll be like his father and run the inn . . . well, we called him, and said to him very quietly, "Who is that young man?" And Vlass answered— Oh please have the goodness not to interrupt, Peter Ivanovitch! You won't tell it right, and anyway you lisp, you've got a tooth in your head that whistles—Well, said Vlass, "That young man," he said, "is a civil servant, an official, travelling from Petersburg to his family in the province of Saratov. His name's Iván Alexándrovitch Hlestakóv, and he behaves very strangely. He's been here two weeks, shows no signs of going, takes everything on credit, and doesn't pay a copek." As he said this, it dawned on me, and I said to Peter Ivanovitch, I said, "Aha!"

DOB. : No! Peter Ivanovitch, I said it first!

(*the Mayor and the rest, who have been displaying increasing impatience, break out, ad lib.*) The devil take the pair of you! What dawned on you?

BOB. : (*unruffled*) Well, perhaps you said " Aha " first, but I said it too.   We both said, " Aha," we said, " Why is he staying here, if his destination's Saratov ? And an official at that ! "

MAYOR : Who ? Which official ?

BOB. : Why ! The one you had the letter about ! The Government Inspector ! (*consternation.*)

MAYOR : (*trying to reassure himself*) What ? God be with us ! That's not him ! It can't be !

DOB. : It must be ! He doesn't go away. He pays no money. Who else could it be ? And he has an official order for post-horses to Saratov !

BOB. : I tell you it's him ! So observant ! He looked at every-thing, even saw that we were eating salmon . . . on account of Peter Ivanovitch's stomach, you know . . . and he came and inspected our plates. It gave me quite a turn !

MAYOR : Lord forgive us, miserable sinners ! What's the number of his room ?

DOB. : Number 4. Under the staircase.

BOB. : The room where the officers had the fight last year.

MAYOR : And how long's he been here ?

DOB. : Two weeks, he came on St. Basil's day.

MAYOR : Two weeks ! Mother of God ! All that time the convicts haven't been fed ! The sergeant's wife's been flogged ! The streets haven't been swept ! The town's like a pothouse ! Disgrace ! Ignominy ! (*clutching temples.*)

CC. : Well, Anton Antonovitch, hadn't we better wait on him in a body ?

MAYOR : No, no ! I'll go alone. I've had some bad turns in the past, and it's come off, and sometimes I've even been thanked into the bargain. Perhaps God will preserve us, even now.   You say he's a young man ?

DOB. : Oh yes. Twenty-three or four at the most.

MAYOR : Good. Young men are easier to handle. There'd be much worse trouble with an old hand. Now, gentlemen, take steps, get things ready, and I'll betake myself alone, or perhaps with Peter Ivanovitch . . . yes, we'll go for a stroll round to the inn, to see how travellers are treated. Oh ! Svistoónov !

[*enter Constable.*]

Go at once to the Police Superintendent, and . . . no !
I shall want you. Tell someone else to go and fetch the
Superintendent, as quickly as possible, and then come back
here. (*Constable runs off.*)

CC. : (*to Judge*) We'd better be going, and get things in order.

JUDGE : What have you got to fear ? You just give out some
clean nightcaps to the patients, and there's an end of it.

CC. : Nightcaps ! We were ordered to give the patients good
oatmeal gruel, and the place stinks of rotten cabbage so
much that you have to hold your nose.

JUDGE : It's just for that reason I'm not worrying. My courthouse smells so, no one will look in at it. But if he had a
look at any of the papers, then life would not be so good.
I've been sitting on the judge's bench here for fifteen years,
and if I had to consult the court records . . . well, I wash
my hands of it ; Solomon himself couldn't tell from them
what was truth and what were lies !

[*the Judge, CC., Sch. Super., and Postmaster go out. In the
doorway they meet the Constable, returning.*]

MAYOR : (*to the Constable*) Is there a cab at the door ?

CONST. : Yes, sir.

MAYOR : Go into the street and . . . no, stop. Go and fetch
. . ., where's the other constable ? I told Próhorov to be
here. Where is he ?

CONST. : He's at his house, he can't go on duty.

MAYOR : Why not ?

CONST. : They brought him in this morning, dead drunk. He's
been soused with two tubfuls of water, but up to now he
hasn't got sober.

MAYOR : (*clutching temples*) Oh ! My God ! My God ! Go quickly
into the street, no . . . run into the other room and fetch
me my sword and new hat. [*exit Constable, left.*]
Now, Peter Ivanovitch we must be getting off.

BOB. : Let me come, too.

MAYOR : No, it's impossible, there's not room in the cab.

BOB. : Never mind that. I'll run behind. I only want to look
through a chink. [*re-enter Constable, with sword and sword-belt,
and a hat-box.*]

MAYOR : (*to Constable, drawing sword*) Go and get the watchmen and . . . good heavens ! Look at the scratches and stains on this sword ! That wretched shopkeeper Abdúlin knows his Mayor's sword's a disgrace ! Any honest fellow would send him a new one ! But these sly people ! They're probably getting ready to complain about me already ! Get the watchmen to bring streets and clean the brooms—devil take it ! You know what I mean. Tell them to sweep the streets, especially near the inn, and sweep them clean, you hear ! And you'd better look out ! I know all about you ! Slipping silver spoons down your boots ! I've got ears ! And your little game with Chernáyev . . . he gave you two yards of cloth for a uniform, and you took the whole roll ! You take more than your rank entitles you to !

[*enter Police Superintendent.*]

Ah ! Stepán Ilyítch ! And where had you vanished to ? It's disgraceful !

PS. : I was here, on the gate.

MAYOR : Well, listen, that official from Petersburg has arrived. What arrangements have you made ?

PS. : As you ordered, I've sent Poogovítsin with the watchmen to sweep the pavements.

MAYOR : And where's Dyerzhímorda ?

PS. : Out with the fire pump.

MAYOR : But Prohorov's drunk. Why do you allow it ?

PS. : God knows ! Yesterday there was a fight on the outskirts, he went to deal with it, and came back drunk.

MAYOR : Now pay attention. Put that tall constable, Poogovitsin, on the bridge, to put up a good appearance. Then pull down that fence by the cobbler's as quick as you can, and put poles with markers as if it was all going to be levelled. The more pulling down you can arrange the better ; it shows the town authorities are active. Oh my God ! I forgot ! Behind that fence there's a pile of stinking rubbish ; forty carts wouldn't take it away ! What a dirty rotten town this is ! You put up some monument, or even a fence, and people come, devil knows where from, and shoot all kinds of filthy rubbish on it ! (*sighs*) Now if this Inspector asks any of the police,

" Are you contented ? " they are to say, " Perfectly contented, your Honour." And if anyone isn't perfectly contented, I'll give 'em something to content them. Oh ! Oh ! I am a sinful man ! I transgress in many ways ! (*picks up hat-box instead of hat ; he has put on his sword during the previous speech*) Oh God ! Keep me out of their clutches this time, and I'll put up the biggest candle you've ever seen ! I'll make every scoundrelly merchant contribute a hundred-weight of wax ! Let's be going, Peter Ivanovitch. (*puts on the box instead of the hat.*)

PS. : (*respectfully*) That's the box, Anton Antonovitch, not the hat.

MAYOR : Very well, it's the box, devil take it. (*putting on his cocked hat*) Now remember, if anyone asks why the hospital chapel hasn't been built that we got the funds for, five years ago, the answer is that it was begun, but it got burnt down. I sent in a report about it. But I suppose some idiot will forget, and say it was never begun ! [*he goes out, then comes back*] And don't let the soldiers run about the streets half naked. The rascals only wear shirts and tunics without any trousers ! [*all go out; the Mayor's wife and daughter come running in from left.*]

ANNA : Where have they gone ? Where have they gone ? (*opening door*) Anton ? Papa ? (*to Marya*) It's all your doing ! Dawdling and rummaging about for pins and necklaces ! (*goes to window, and leans out, calling*) Anton ! Papa ! Where are you off to ? What ? Has he come ? The Government Inspector of course ! What's he like ? Has he a moustache ? Is he handsome ?

MAYOR : (*below*) Bye'n'bye, m'dear ! Bye'n'bye !

ANNA : Bye'n'bye ! That's news, that is ! What is he ? A colonel ? (*sound of one horse cab driving off*) He's gone. I'll remember this. (*mimicking daughter*) " Mummy ! Mummy ! Wait ! Fasten my necklace at the back ! " Now we've not found out anything. All through your maddening conceit ! Because you heard the Postmaster was here, you had to start preening yourself in front of a mirror. You think he's courting you, and all the time he makes faces when your back's turned !

34

MARYA : Well, never mind, Mummy. We shall know all about it in an hour or two.

ANNA : An hour or two! Thank you kindly! Why not say a month or two? (*leaning out of window*) Hey! Avdotya! Avdotya! What? Have you found out who's come? No? What a fool! Anton waved you away? That makes no difference, you ought to have stopped him and found out everything! Stuff and nonsense! They drove off quickly? Well run after the cab! Go on! Run! Look through a chink and find out everything! What colour eyes he's got, and whether he's got a moustache! And come back here at once! Go on! D'you hear? Hurry! Hurry! Hurry!
(*She is leaning out of the window shouting at the top of her voice when*)

THE CURTAIN FALLS.

ACT II SCENE 1

The scene is a room at the inn; it is a poky little room, with only one small window; there is a table with an empty bottle on it, a bed, a travelling trunk, a pair of top-boots in the corner; two or three chairs; at curtain-rise Yosif, Hlestakov's servant, is sprawling on his master's bed.

YOSIF : Ouch! I'm so hungry my belly's rumbling like a regiment of drummers! And we're not going to get home at this rate! What's to be done? Two months since we left Petersburg! Well, we've chucked money away on the road, chucked it away like water, we have, and now we sit here with our tail between our legs. What's to do now? There'd have been enough and plenty for the fares, but, you know, everywhere we stop we have to show off. (*scratches himself, imitating Hlestakov*) " Hey, Yosif. Run along and book me rooms. The best, remember! And order me the very best dinner they have! I can't look at common food, I must have the very best! " And him a junior copying clerk! And, of course, he makes friends with the other travellers, and then, out come the cards, and they play till he gets cleaned out! Eh! It's a dog's life. Better to live in the country. It's dull, but there's not all this trouble. You get yourself a good fat country wench, and spend your time lying over the stove, and eating pies. Yet, when all's said and done there's nothing to touch life in Petersburg. So long as you've got money to spend, it's a fine life, a dainty life! Theatres! Dancing dogs! Any thing you've a mind to! Everybody speaks so nice and refined, pretty near as good as the gentry even! We go round the bazaars; the shopkeepers all call us " Honorable Sir." We sit in the special seats on the ferry-boats. Sometimes there'll be officers full of the regimental gossip, or another time a pretty lady's maid may come tripping by. (*laughs and shakes his head*) E-eh! It's a fine life! Everybody treats you as if you was a gentleman. When you get tired you hail a cab and take your ease like a nobleman, and if you don't want to pay, well, you don't! Now it's different. Well, it's not my fault. My master never could keep a grip on money. Sometimes we live on the fat of the land, and other times, like now, we fair shrink with hunger. What can I do? When his father sends him money, instead of keeping a tight hold on it—whee-eesh! Off he goes on the spree! Everywhere by cab! Theatre tickets every day! And in a week, it's all gone, and he sends me to pop his new suit! One time, everything went, down to our last shirt and he only had a tail-coat and an overcoat left! S'true, so help me! And all beautiful English cloth! One coat cost him a hundred and fifty roubles, and it went for twenty ! And as for the trousers they go for nothing ! It's all because he won't stick to business, instead of swaggering up and down the Nevsky, or losing all his money at cards ! If his old father only knew, he'd lift up his little shirt tails, and give him such a whacking he'd be rubbing his behind for a week, even though he is a copying-clerk in the Civil Service ! If you've got a job, then do it, I say ! (*groans*) I'm so hungry I could eat the whole world ! (*footsteps off*) Somebody's coming ! Sounds like him ! [*gets off the bed; enter Hlestakov.*]

HLEST. : Here, take these. (*handing Yosif his hat and cane.*) Have you been rolling on my bed again ?

YOSIF : Why should I roll on your bed ? Think I've never seen a bed before ?

HLEST. : That's a lie ! you have been rolling on it. Look, it's all rumpled.

YOSIF : What's that to me ? Don't I know what a bed's for ? I've got legs, I stand on them. What's your bed to me ?

HLEST. : (*pacing the room*) Look and see if there's any tobacco in that jar.

YOSIF : How should there be any ? You smoked the last four days ago.

HLEST. : (*pacing up and down, finally says in a very loud and determined voice*) Hey ! Listen, Yosif.

YOSIF : What's your wish ?

HLEST. : (*loudly, but not quite so determined*) Go down there.

YOSIF : Where ?

HLEST. : Downstairs. (*not at all loud or determined now, but beseeching*) Downstairs in the kitchen. Tell them they must send me some dinner.

YOSIF : I'd rather not.

HLEST. : How dare you ! You oaf !

YOSIF : Very well. But all the same, if I do go, nothing will happen. The landlord said he wouldn't serve you any more meals till you'd paid him.

HLEST. : Nonsense ! How dare he refuse ?

YOSIF : Well, he says he'll go to the Mayor, and tell him this is the third week you've been here without paying. " You and your master," he says, " you're swindlers, and your master's a rogue. Spongers and scoundrels," he says.

HLEST. : And you enjoy telling me all this, you brute !

YOSIF : He says : " You people come here, live at ease, run up a bill you can't pay, and then refuse to budge. I'm going straight to the police," he says, " with a complaint, and I'm not joking either, and you'll end up in jail."

HLEST. : That's enough, idiot ! Go and tell him, the low animal !

YOSIF : I'd better call him for you to speak to him.

HLEST. : I don't want to see him ; go and tell him yourself !

YOSIF : Yes, right, Sir.

HLEST. : Go on, devil take it. Fetch the landlord ! [*Yosif goes off.*] It's awful to be so hungry. I thought I could walk it off, but damnation take it, I'm as hungry as ever. If only I hadn't had such a spree in Penza, there'd have been enough to get home on. That infantry captain certainly took me in ! The way he piled up game after game ! The brute ! He only sat down for a quarter of an hour, but he licked me clean ! I wish I could have had another go at him, but there was no chance. What a dirty little hole this town is ! These fleabitten shopkeepers won't part with anything on tick ! A mean lot ! (*walks up and down whistling tunes of the day, " Roberta," " The Marriage of Figaro," and then anything that comes into his head*).

[re-enter Yosif and the waiter.]

WAITER : The landlord has sent me to ask your pleasure.

HLEST. : Good-day, my friend. How are you ?

WAITER : Well, I thank God.

HLEST. : How's the hotel business these days ?

WAITER : Very good, God be praised.

HLEST. : Many travellers ?

WAITER : Sufficient.

HLEST. : Listen, friend. They've brought me no dinner yet. Please hurry up with it, as quickly as possible—I've something I must do after dinner.

WAITER : The landlord said he would not serve you anything more. He was going to-day to complain to the Mayor.

HLEST. : What about ? Consider, my dear fellow, I have to eat ! Or else I should get very thin ! I need something to eat very badly. I'm not joking !

WAITER : Well, he said : " I shall serve him no more meals till he pays for what he's had." That was what he said.

HLEST. : You must explain to him, persuade him.

WAITER : But what shall I say ?

HLEST. : Well, you must talk to him very seriously, explain that I have to eat. The money doesn't matter . . . He's a peasant, he thinks it's nothing to go a day without eating. A fine idea !

WAITER : All right, I'll tell him. [*exeunt waiter and Yosif.*]

HLEST. : It'll be frightful, though, if he won't give me anything to eat ! I never knew you could be as hungry as this before. I might sell some clothes for ready cash ; a few pairs of trousers, say. No ! Better to go hungry than not arrive home in Petersburg clothes ! Pity Joachim wouldn't let me hire that chaise. It would have been devilish fine to go home in my own chaise, and go visiting the landowners, and drive up to the foot of the steps, with the lanterns burning, and Yosif in livery perched up behind ! I can just imagine everybody getting excited, and asking, " Who is it ? What is it ? " And the lacquey would go in (*stretching himself and representing the lacquey*) " Ivan Alexandrovitch Hlestakov, from Petersburg ; are they at home ? " They're only bumpkins, they wouldn't know what that meant ! If some goose of a landowner went to see them, he'd charge straight into the drawing-room like a bear. You make a bee-line for some pretty daughter. " Allow me . . ." Ugh ! It's sickening to be so hungry !

[*enter Yosif, followed by the waiter.*]

YOSIF : They're bringing some dinner.

HLEST. : (*claps his hands and jumps into a chair*) Dinner ! Dinner ! Dinner !

WAITER : (*with plates and napkin, etc.*) This is the last time you'll be served . . . that's the landlord's orders.

HLEST. : The landlord ! The landlord ! The devil take the landlord ! What have you got there ?

WAITER : Soup and roast fowl.

HLEST. : Only two courses ?

WAITER : That's all.

HLEST. : It's ridiculous ! I won't have that ! Go and tell him, tell him it's impossible ! It's not enough !

WAITER : The landlord says it's too much.

HLEST. : And why no sauce ?

WAITER : There is no sauce.

HLEST. : Why not ? I saw them making a lot, when I came by the kitchen. And there were two little men in the dining-room this morning eating salmon and lots of nice things.

WAITER : Well, there is, and then again there isn't.

HLEST. : Why not ?

WAITER : There just isn't.

HLEST. : Isn't there any salmon or cutlets, or fish ?

WAITER : They're for the better-class customers.

HLEST. : You fool, you !

WAITER : Yes, sir.

HLEST. : You dirty pig ! How is it they can eat, and not me ? Why am I not treated the same ? Aren't they travellers just like me ?

WAITER : Well, we all know they're not the same.

HLEST. : Why not ?

WAITER : They're the usual sort, to be sure ! It's like this, you see, they pay !

HLEST. : You fool ! I shan't waste my breath on you ! (*pours out the soup and begins his dinner*) What sort of soup is this ? You've simply put dirty water in the cup ! There's no flavour ; it just stinks ! I won't have this soup ; bring me another kind !

WAITER : Certainly, sir ! The landlord said if you didn't like it, you needn't have it.

HLEST. : (*immediately protecting his soup from removal*) Leave it, leave it, you numskull ! You may be used to treating other people like this, but I warn you, I'm not that sort of a man ! I won't have it ! (*still drinking his soup*) Good Heavens ! What soup ! I don't think there's anyone else in the world who would swallow such soup ! Ugh ! Look at the feathers floating in it ! Give me the roast. (*carving fowl*) Good God ! What a brute of a fowl ! There's a little soup left there, Yosif, you can have. Roast chicken ! That's not a roast chicken !

WAITER : What is it ?

HLEST. : The devil only knows what it is, but it isn't a chicken ! Thieves ! Rabble ! I wonder what they're having now ? Your jaws ache if you eat a mouthful of this ! (*picking his teeth*) The beasts ! This is like the bark of a tree, long and stringy, you can't get it out ! It will make my teeth black ! Robbers ! Isn't there anything else ?

WAITER : No.

HLEST. : The idlers ! The scum ! No sauce or pudding ? Just fleecing travellers, that's what it is !

[*the waiter and Yosif clear away and go out.*]

I feel as if I'd had nothing at all ! Only enough to whet an appetite ! If I had a few coppers I could send out and buy some buns.

[*re-enter Yosif.*]

YOSIF : The mayor's come ! He's down there making enquiries and asking about you !

HLEST. : (*scared*) What ? That beastly landlord has sent in a complaint already ! What if he has me dragged to prison ? Well, if they treat me like a gentleman, I might . . . but no ! I won't go ! There are all sorts of officers and people walking about outside and of course I've been setting the fashion, and flirting with the daughter of the shop-keeper next door. No, I couldn't ! I won't go ! Who is this Mayor ? How dare he ? Does he think I'm a workman ? (*draws himself up and looks very brave*) I shall tell him, I shall say : " How dare you do this to me ? How dare you ? "

[*the door-handle turns, and his voice tails off ; he cringes, and tries to hide, but the room is too bare ; the Mayor enters, and seeing Hlest. stops ; both are terrified, and they look at each other without moving, in silence, for some moments, goggle-eyed; the Mayor recovers first, and stands to attention in the presence of his supposedly superior officer.*]

MAYOR : I have the honour to wish you " Good Day." [*Dobchinsky creeps in.*]

HLEST. : My compliments !

MAYOR : Pardon my intrusion !

HLEST. : Not at all.

MAYOR : It is my duty, as the chief authority in this town to see that travellers and people of rank suffer no inconvenience.

HLEST. : (*stammering a little at first, but nearly shouting toward the end of the speech*) But what am I to do ? I haven't done anything ! I will pay ! [*Bobchinsky peeps round the door.*] It's all the innkeeper's fault ! He gives me meat as hard as a beam, and the soup . . . ! Heaven knows what he puts into it ! I've had to throw it out of the window. He's been starving me for several days ! And such tea . . . ! It tastes of fish, it's not tea at all ! A fine state of affairs ! Why should I go to . . . ?

MAYOR : (*intimidated*) Forgive me ! I'm exceedingly sorry ! It really isn't my fault. Our market is noted for its excellent beef. The tradespeople are sober, honest people, of very good repute. Indeed I don't know where he gets such stuff. But as you are not comfortable, permit me to suggest that you move to other quarters.

HLEST. : No, I won't go ! I know what you mean by other quarters ; you mean prison ! What right have you ? How dare you ? I—I—I am a Government servant ! In Petersburg ! (*plucking up courage*) I—I—I'll go—

MAYOR : (*aside*) God in Heaven ! He knows everything ! Those cursed shopkeepers !

HLEST. : (*getting bolder*) Not if you came here with a regiment, I wouldn't go ! I shall go straight to the Minister ! (*bangs fist on the table*) You ! You !

MAYOR : (*shivering all over, and nearly grovelling*) Mercy ! Have mercy on me ! Don't ruin me ! My wife—little children— ! Don't make me wretched for ever !

HLEST. : No ! I shan't go ! A fine idea ; just because you have a wife and children I must go to prison ! The very idea ! [*Bob. peeps round the door, and draws back, terrified.*] No, I humbly thank you ! I'm not going !

MAYOR : (*trembling*) It was my inexperience, God knows it was only my inexperience ! And the miserable pittance I get ! You can judge for yourself : my official salary doesn't pay for the tea and sugar ! If I have taken bribes they were only little ones, something for the table, or a bit of cloth for a suit ! As for the sergeant's wife and the story that I had her flogged, it's all lies ! Slander ! It's an invention of my enemies ! Such people ! I go in daily fear of assassination !

HLEST. : They are nothing to do with me. (*thinking*) I don't know why you tell me all this, about your enemies and sergeants' wives. A sergeant's wife is one thing, but you daren't try to flog me . . . that's altogether too big a job for you ! I should think so ! I shall pay, I shall pay my bill when I have the money, but until then I shall have to stay here, because I haven't a copek.

MAYOR : (*aside :*) The clever devil ! What a hint ! You can make what you can of it ! There's no knowing how that's to be taken ! What will be, will be ; I'll try him out. (*aloud:*) If you are in any little financial difficulty, perhaps, or any other difficulty I am at your service. It is my duty to aid travellers in any way.

HLEST. : Yes, yes. Let me have a loan. Then I can pay the innkeeper at once. Two hundred roubles would do, or even less.

MAYOR : Two hundred roubles exactly, pray do not trouble to count it.

HLEST. : I'm most obliged. I'll send it back as soon as I reach my country estate. I see you are a gentleman.

MAYOR : (*aside :*) Thank God ! He's taken it ! Things will go smoothly after all, and I managed to give him 400 instead of 200.

HLEST. : Hey ! Yosif ! [*enter Y.*] Fetch the waiter ! [*exit Y.*] (*to Mayor and Dob.*) But why are you standing ? (*they are reluctant to sit*) Please sit down, I beg ! (*with some reluctance, they sit*) I see now the straightforwardness and generosity of your character, but I confess, I thought you had come to take . . . (*to Dob. who had risen.*) Sit down ! [*Bob. peeps round door and listens.*]

MAYOR : (*aside :*) I must be bolder. He wants to be considered incognito. Very well, we'll make small talk and pretend we don't know who he is. (*aloud :*) I was strolling about on public business, with Peter Ivanovitch Dobchinsky here, who is a landowner in the town, and we turned into the

43

inn, on purpose to find out how they treat travellers here. I'm not like some Mayors who care nothing about such things. Over and above my duty, I like to see to it, in Christian love of mankind, that every mortal who passes this way is received kindly, and in this case, I have the reward of making a pleasant acquaintance.

HLEST. : I am very glad also. But for you I should have had to remain here a long time. I had no idea how I could pay my bill.

MAYOR : (*aside :*) A fine tale ! No idea how he could pay his bill ! (*aloud :*) May I ask where you are travelling to ?

HLEST. : I am going to my own estate in the province of Sarátov.

MAYOR : (*aside :*) Province of Sarátov !—And he says it without a blush !—You've got to have your ears cocked dealing with him. (*aloud :*) An excellent idea ! Though in travelling, there are pros and cons. There is the mental diversion, of course, but on the other hand the annoyances and delays of the road, shortage of horses, and so on. But I take it you are travelling for your own pleasure ?

HLEST. : No, my father has sent for me. The old man is annoyed that I haven't been promoted in the service before now. He thinks as soon as you get to Petersburg they stick the Order of Vladímir in your buttonhole. I ought to have sent him to bustle about the office !

MAYOR : (*aside :*) What fibs he tells, dragging in his old father ! (*aloud :*) Do you intend to stay there long ?

HLEST. : Really, I don't know. You see, my father is as stupid and obstinate as a block of wood, the old fool ! I shall tell him straight out, " Say what you like, but I cannot *live* away from Petersburg. Why must I ruin my life, living among peasants ? My heart is athirst for truth and light ! "

MAYOR : (*aside :*) What a liar ! Fairy tale after fairy tale, and all so consistent ! What a puny nasty-looking fellow ! I could crack him under my finger-nail ! I must get him talking. (*aloud :*) As you were pleased to say just now, what can one do in these country places ? Take me for example ; tossing through sleepless nights, growing old in my country's service, grudging no efforts or toil in the service of my fellow-men, but as for recognition, who knows when it will come ? (*looking round the room*) This room seems somewhat damp.

HLEST. : It's a filthy room, and the bugs in it, I never saw their like.

MAYOR : Dear me ! Such a distinguished guest, to be made to suffer, from what ? from a lot of wretched bugs, that ought never to have been born ! Don't you think it is dark in this room ?

HLEST. : Yes, it is dark. But the landlord refuses to give me candles. Now and then when I want to do something, to read a little, or I feel inspired to write, I cannot ; it is too dark, too dark !

MAYOR : If I might venture to beg you . . . but no ! I am unworthy !

HLEST. : To beg what ?

MAYOR : No ! No ! I am unworthy to ask it ! Unworthy !

HLEST. : But what is it ?

MAYOR : If I may venture. . . . I have a delightful room in my house, . . . sunny . . . pleasant. . . . But no ! It would be too great an honour ! Do not be angry, it was the simplicity of my heart that made me offer it !

HLEST. : On the contrary, it would give me great pleasure. It would be much nicer in a private house, than in this low tavern !

MAYOR : I am very glad ; and my wife will be delighted ! That is my nature ! I was hospitable even as a child, and of course when the guest is such a distinguished one ! But pray do not think I say that out of flattery ! That is a vice unknown to me ; I speak from a full heart.

HLEST. : I am very much in your debt. I am the same, I detest two-faced people. Your candour and cordiality appeal to me, and for my part, I confess, I ask for nothing from others, but sympathy and consideration.

[*enter Yosif and the waiter.*]

WAITER : (*very respectful*) Your Honour wishes for something ?

HLEST. : My bill !

WAITER : I gave it you again this morning.

HLEST. : I can't look after all your stupid bills ! How much is it ?

WAITER : Well, the first day you had the dinner, the second you only wanted salmon. . . .

HLEST. : Imbecile ! No need to go through all that ! How much do I owe in all ?

MAYOR : Do not trouble about such a matter, sir. He can wait. (*to the waiter*) Clear off ; the money will be sent to you.

HLEST. : (*puts away money. Bob. is again seen listening*) Yes, that is best. [*exit waiter.*]

MAYOR : You might like to inspect some of the institutions, both public and private, in our town.

HLEST. : You mean . . . ?

MAYOR : You would see how things are done here. We have everything in very good order.

HLEST. : I should be delighted. I am at your service. (*Bob. peeping.*)

MAYOR : If you like we could go from here to the district school, to study our teaching methods.

HLEST. : Certainly.

MAYOR : From there to the police station and the town prison, to see how we deal with criminals.

HLEST. : (*suspicions reviving*) But why the prison ? The charitable institutions would be better.

MAYOR : As you please. Would you prefer to use your own carriage, or take a cab ?

HLEST. : I would rather accompany you in a cab.

MAYOR : (*to Dob.*) In that case, Peter Ivanovitch, there will be no room for you.

DOB. : That doesn't matter.

MAYOR : (*quietly, to Dob.*) Listen. You must take two notes for me, as fast as you can. One to Zemlyanika at the hospital, the other to my wife. (*to Hlest.*) May I beg your permission to write a few lines to my wife, to tell her to prepare the reception for our honoured guest ?

HLEST. : Certainly. . . . There is ink here, but no paper. Why not use the back of this bill ? (*which he straightway produces from his pocket.*)

MAYOR : Yes, that will do. (*writes while talking half to himself*) We'll see how things will go after a glass or two of vodka. Then I've got some of our home-grown Madeira ; it's not an elegant wine, but it would topple an elephant. (*having finished notes, he hands them to Dob. who goes toward the door, but at this moment the door comes off its hinges, and Bobchinsky, who has been listening at the keyhole during the whole scene, comes flying in on top of it ; all utter startled exclamations. Bob. picks himself up.*)

HLEST. : Haven't you hurt yourself anywhere ? [*exit Dob.*]

BOB. : Not at all, not at all, I assure you. Pray don't concern yourself. Only a slight blow on my nose. I shall go to Christian Ivanovitch ; he has a plaster, you know, that's very good. You put it on, and (*bus. arms*) it goes !

MAYOR : (*looking daggers at Bob.*) It is nothing. Shall we go ? I'll tell your man to bring your luggage. (*to Yosif*) My good man, bring it to my house, the Mayor's house, anyone will show you. (*to Hlest. at door*) No, after you, I beg. (*waves Hlest. through and follows him, but rounds on Bob., before going out*) You ! You ! Couldn't you have done your knockabout performance somewhere else ? Coming sprawling in like the devil knows what ! (*pushes Bob. through the door and follows him out, muttering imprecations as*)

THE CURTAIN FALLS.

ACT II SCENE 2

The room in the house of the Mayor; afternoon of the same day; the Mayor's wife and daughter are standing by the window in the same position as at the end of Act I.

ANNA : Now you see ! We've been waiting a whole hour, and all through your silly affectation ! You were all dressed and ready, but no ! You still had to rummage about for frills and wouldn't listen at all ! What a nuisance ! Not a soul in sight, just as if to annoy me. As if everything had died.

MARYA : Now really, mummy, you'll know all about it in two minutes ! Avdotya must be hurrying back this minute. (*leans out of window*) Mummy, mummy, who's that coming, look, at the end of the street ?

ANNA : Who's coming ? You're always imagining things ! There ! Yes, there is somebody, who is it ? A little man in a frock coat. Who is it ? Oh ! What a nuisance, I can't tell.

MARYA : It's Dobchinsky, mummy.

ANNA : Dobchinsky indeed ! How such moonshine comes into your head ! It's obviously not Dobchinsky. (*waving handkerchief*) Hey ! You ! Come here ! Quickly !

MARYA : Really, mummy, it is Dobchinsky.

ANNA : You say that on purpose to contradict me. I tell you, it's not Dobchinsky.

MARYA : Well, look, mummy, you see it really is Dobchinsky, I told you so !

ANNA : Yes ! Well, I can see now. It is Dobchinsky ! What are you arguing about ? (*shrieking out of the window*) Quicker ! Quicker ! What are you dawdling about for ? Where are they ? What ? Well, go on ; tell me ! Yes, I can hear you. Get on and tell me ! What ! Very stern ? And Anton ? My husband ? (*retreating from window*) What an idiot ! He can't tell me till he gets up here !

[*enter Dobchinsky, sprinting.*]

Now tell me ! Aren't you ashamed of yourself ? I relied on you as a decent man ! Everybody suddenly goes running off, and you as well, and here I've been for hours without any proper news ! And I still am ! Aren't you ashamed ? And I stood godmother to your Ványa and Liza, and this is how you treat me for it !

DOB. : My goodness ! I've run so fast to pay my respects to you, I'm quite out of breath ! How do you do ? Márya (*gulp*) Antónovna !

MARYA : Good afternoon, Peter Ivanovitch.

ANNA : Now get on ! Tell me what happened ?

DOB. : Anton Antonovitch gave me a note for you.

48

ANNA : But who is he ? A general ?

DOB. : No. He isn't a general, but he'd make way for no general ! Such learning ! Such grand manners !

ANNA : Then he's the one my husband had the letter about ?

DOB. : (*grandly*) The very same ! And I discovered him ! I and Peter Ivanovitch !

ANNA : Well, tell us, tell us all about it.

DOB. : Well, God be praised, everything is quite all right. At the beginning he received Anton Antonovitch a little sternly. Yes ! He was very angry and said that everything in the hotel was bad, that he wouldn't go to prison just for that. But then when he found that Anton Antonovitch was not to blame and got into closer conversation with him he changed his mind, and then, thank God, all went well. They've gone now to look at the hospital . . . Anton Antonovitch really did think at first there might have been a secret report about him ; and I was a little afraid myself.

ANNA : What had you got to be afraid of ? You aren't in the Service.

DOB. : Well, you know, when such a great man speaks, one does feel very nervous.

ANNA : All that doesn't matter. What's he like himself ? Old or young ?

DOB. : Oh ! A young man ! A young man ! About twenty-three. But he speaks like an old man. So grave ! So dignified ! " There's an old head on young shoulders," I said. " Let it be so," he said, " I will go there, and there." (*gesticulating with arms, very dignified*) And all so elegant ! " I like to read a little," he said, " and I write, you know, I write. But it is a pity this room is so dark ! "

ANNA : But what's he like to look at ? Fair haired or dark ?

DOB. : No, more auburn. And such quick darting eyes !

ANNA : I must read this note. " I hasten to inform you, my love, that my condition was truly dismal, but trusting in God's mercy for two pickled cucumbers and half a portion of caviare, one rouble and twenty-five copeks." I don't understand. What have pickled cucumbers and caviare got to do with it ?

DOB. : He wrote it hastily on an old piece of paper ; a bill, I think.

ANNA : Yes, that's it. . . . . " trusting in God's mercy, it seems that it will all end well. Prepare as quickly as you can, a room for our distinguished guest, the one with the yellow wall-paper. Don't trouble to have anything extra for dinner, as we shall have something with Artemy Filipovitch at the hospital, but order more wine. Tell Abdulin the wine merchant to send in his very best, or else I'll turn his cellar inside out! I kiss your little hand, my love, and I remain, ever your Anton Skvóznik-Dmuhanóvsky." My goodness! Now we've got to hurry! Hey! Who's there? Mishka!

DOB. : (*goes and calls through the door*) Mishka! Mishka!

[*enter Mishka.*]

ANNA : Listen, run to Abdulin's, wait, I'll give you a note. (*sits at table, writing and giving orders*) Give this note to Sidor the coachman, and tell him to hurry there and bring back the wine. And go yourself at once and tidy up that room (*pointing to exit, right*) for a visitor. Put in a wash-basin, plenty of towels, soap and everything.

DOB. : Well now, Anna Andréyevna, I shall run along to see him inspecting the hospital.

ANNA : Be off, then, be off! I'm not stopping you.

[*exit Dobchinsky.*]

Now, Máshenka, we must think carefully what we are going to wear! He's a Petersburg dandy; Heaven forbid he should laugh at us up his sleeve! You'd better wear your pale blue with the flounces.

MARYA : Oh, Mummy! The pale blue? (*stamps*) I hate it! Lyapkin-Tyapkin's wife always goes about in pale blue, and the Zemlyanika girl never takes it off! Much better if I wore the flowered one!

ANNA : The flowered one! You only say that to spite me! But perhaps it will be best for you to wear your flowered dress, because then I can wear my primrose. I'm very fond of primrose; it suits me.

MARYA : Oh, Mummy! You look dreadful in primrose.

ANNA : I look dreadful in primrose?

MARYA : Yes. Of course you do. You must have dark eyes to wear primrose.

ANNA : A fine idea ! And aren't my eyes dark ? Of course they are ! Very dark. What rubbish you talk ! How shouldn't they be dark, when I always tell my fortune by the Queen of Clubs ?

MARYA : You're more like the Queen of Hearts.

ANNA : Rubbish ! Absolute rubbish ! I never was like the Queen of Hearts ! (*goes off hurriedly with Marya, still talking*) Such nonsense ! Queen of Hearts ! What will you think of next ? [*Mishka opens the door left and sweeps. Yosif appears in the centre door, with Hlestakov's trunk on his back.*]

YOSIF : Where does this go ?

MISHKA : This way, daddy, this way.

YOSIF : Wait a minute, let me get my breath. An empty belly makes anything heavy.

MISHKA : Tell me, is the general coming here soon ?

YOSIF : What general ?

MISHKA : Why, your master, of course.

YOSIF : My master ? How long's he been a general ?

MISHKA : Well, isn't he a general ?

YOSIF : He's a general ; inside out and back to front.

MISHKA : Is that more or less than a proper general ?

YOSIF : More, much more.

MISHKA : Oh, oh. That's why there's all the fuss in the house.

YOSIF : Listen, my lad. I can see you're a sensible chap. Can you get me something to eat ?

MISHKA : There's nothing ready for you yet, daddy. It isn't plain food you'll be having, I can tell you. When your master sits down to table, you'll get the same as he does.

YOSIF : What might you have ready now, in the way of plain food ?

MISHKA : Cabbage broth, meat pie, and pudding.

YOSIF : Well, get me some of that, cabbage broth, meat pie, and pudding. I could eat anything. Come on, let's pick up this box. Which room ? That one ?

MISHKA : Yes, in here. [*they both go off, with the trunk, into the room prepared for Hlestakov ; two Constables come on and open the double doors ; enter Hlestakov, the Mayor just behind him,*] *the Charity Commissioner, the School Superintendent, then Dobchinsky and Bobchinsky, the latter with plaster on his nose; the Mayor points out to the Constables a piece of paper on the floor, which they both run to pick up, bustling about; a tremendous show is being put on; all but Hlestakov are at full stretch.*]

HLEST. : A fine institution. I liked it very much. It's not every town that takes such pains to show travellers round. In other towns I have passed through they have shown me nothing.

MAYOR : Ah! In other towns, I venture to suggest, the Mayors and officials are more concerned about, shall I say, their own interests, but here none of us has a thought for anything but our one aim; to earn the good opinion of the authorities by vigilance, good government, and honesty!

HLEST. : That was a very good lunch. I quite over-ate myself. Do you have such a good meal every day?

MAYOR : Oh no! It was prepared specially for our distinguished guest.

HLEST. : I like a good dinner. But then that's what life is for— to pick the flowers of pleasure. What was the name of that fish we had?

CC. : (*scurries up*) Labardán,* sir.

HLEST. : Labardan? A most delicate flavour. Where was it we lunched? At the hospital, wasn't it?

CC. : Yes.

HLEST. : Where all those beds were. Had all the patients recovered? I didn't see very many.

CC. : There are only ten left now, the rest have completely recovered. It always happens like that, things are so well organised, the management is so good. You know, from the day I took control, the patients have got better—it may seem incredible, but they've always got better like flies! They're hardly inside the place, before they're better! It's not so much a matter of medicines, as of honesty, cleanliness, and good order.

MAYOR : (*jealously elbowing him aside :*) Ah! But I assure you, that's

---

* " Labardan " was an unusual name for salt cod (from Aberdeen). Hlest. thinks it a rare delicacy. If desired, " codfish " may be used instead.

nothing compared to the burdens of a Mayor, nerve-racking, simply nerve-racking ! So many things to be kept in mind, nothing must be overlooked . . . cleanliness . . . good order . . . repair and maintenance. The wisest man might be perplexed at times, but with the help of God, all goes well. Some Mayors, now, might put their own interests first, but, you know, even when I lie down to sleep, I think constantly, " Oh, Lord God, if I could earn the thanks of the authorities for my zeal, that would be enough. If they reward my services, or not, at least I shall always have the satisfaction of work well done ! " So long as the town is well kept, the streets clean, the convicts looked after, drunkenness kept down, what more could I want ? Truly, I want no honours ! They're alluring, I grant you, but what are they compared to a virtuous life ? Dust and ashes ! That's all.

cc. : *(aside :)* How he lays it on ! The good-for-nothing ! God certainly gave him the gift of the gab !

hlest. : You're quite right. I like to philosophise myself, sometimes in prose, and another time I may toss off a poem.

bob. : *(to Dob.)* That's apt, Peter Ivanovitch, very apt. Such clever remarks . . . it's easy to see he's a most learned man !

hlest. : But tell me, haven't you any diversions, any amusements ? Don't you ever foregather round a card-table ?

mayor : *(aside :)* Ah ! We know whose garden you're throwing stones into ! *(aloud :)* God forbid, there is no mention of such things here ! I've never held a card in my hand ! I don't even know how to play ! I can't even look at a card, it makes me ill ! Once I had to amuse some children, and built them a house of cards and when I went to bed it gave me a nightmare ! How some people can waste so much precious time on them ! I use it better, in the Government service.

hlest. : Oh no ! It all depends on how you look at it ! If you lose, you must double your stake. I think a game is sometimes very engrossing.

[enter Anna and Marya, freshly gowned.]

mayor : Allow me to present my family ; my wife and daughter.

HLEST. : (*bowing*) How happy it makes me to have the pleasure of meeting you !

ANNA : It is a greater honour for us to meet such an illustrious guest.

HLEST. : (*taking on airs*) Oh, but forgive me; on the contrary, the honour is mine.

ANNA : Your Honour is pleased to say that as a compliment. But I beg you to sit down.

HLEST. : But what happiness to stand beside you ! Still, if you really wish it, I will sit down. How happy I should be to sit, by you !

(*they sit on the same sofa.*)

ANNA : I suppose country life must be very dull to you, after Petersburg ?

HLEST. : It is extremely unpleasant. Having got used to living, comprenez-vous,* in the haut monde, suddenly to find one-self on the road ; dirty inns, ignorance, uncouth people ! But of course, when I fall into such hands as yours, that makes up for everything ! (*he is playing up to Anna, and laying it on.*)

ANNA : But still, it must be unpleasant for so great a . . .

HLEST. : At this moment, I assure you, it's very pleasant indeed.

ANNA : You do me too much honour ; more than I merit.

HLEST. : Nothing in the world is too good for you.

ANNA : But I live in the country ! Your Petersburg ladies . . .

HLEST. : Ah ! The country ! The country has its little hills and brooks . . . ! But who would compare it with Petersburg ! Ah ! Petersburg ! C'est la vie ! Perhaps you are thinking that I'm just a copying clerk ! No, I'm on very friendly terms with the chief of my department. He often comes into my office, claps me on the back, and says, " Let's go and have dinner, old man ! " I just pop into the outer office to tell them what to be getting on with. There's a man there who does nothing but write letters for me (*bus., writing*

---

* The French phrases which Hlestakov uses in this scene are simply scraps which he has picked up, like a child, and which he uses to impress people, since, like many half-educated people of those days, he despises the vernacular. To bring out this point the phrases should be pronounced with a strong English accent.

rapidly) just like that, all day ! But why are you standing, gentlemen ?

OFFICIALS : (*ad lib.*) We know our place. We know our rank. Please don't concern yourself, sir. We will stand.

HLEST. : Rank or no rank, gentlemen, please be seated. (*they sit*) I never stand on ceremony. In fact, I do my best to be inconspicuous, to pass unnoticed. But I find it's impossible, quite impossible ! Whenever I go anywhere, the word soon goes round, " Look ! There goes Ivan Alexandrovitch ! " One night I was taken for the Commander-in-Chief himself . The sentry called out the guard to present arms. Of course at the time I wondered why, but an officer who's a great friend of mine told me afterwards, " You know, old boy, they were convinced it was the C.-in-C. ! "

ANNA : Well, I never !

HLEST. : I'm great friends with all the pretty actresses ! I have written a few trifles for the stage, you see. I meet all the best writers. Pushkin and I are great friends ! Whenever I see him I say, " Well, Pushkin, old man, how goes it ? " And he calls out, " Bearing up, old boy, bearing up ! " He's a great character !

ANNA : So you write ! It must be wonderful to be an author ! Do you write bits for the magazines ?

HLEST : Oh yes ! I've written a lot of stuff ! " The Marriage of Figaro," " Robert the Devil," " Norma," that's just a few. I can't remember all the names. It's just a sideline. I'm not keen on writing, but the theatre managers come and beg me : " Write us another play, old chap ; we need a success." And I think to myself it might be rather fun ! And I spend an evening on it, and voilà ! a new play ! It astounds everybody ! Thoughts and ideas come tumbling from my brain ! Everything published by Baron Brambeus,* The Frigate Hope, and the Moscow Daily Telegraph ! All mine !

ANNA : Well now ! So you are Brambeus !

HLEST. : Yes, I correct all their articles. They pay me 40,000 a year for that.

---

* These were the pseudonym of a successful novelist, a best-selling novel, and a newspaper, respectively. To Hlest. they are all just names, with some sort of literary connexion.

ANNA : Then " Youri Miloslavsky " must be your work, too ?

HLEST. : Yes, that's another.

ANNA : There ! I knew at once !

MARYA : But Mummy ! It says on the cover that a Mr. Zagoskin wrote it !

ANNA : I knew you would have to argue about it, whatever I said !

HLEST. : But please don't scold your charming daughter. She's quite right ; Zagoskin did write it. But there's another "Youri Miloslavsky " that I wrote.

ANNA : Well, I know it was yours I read. What wonderful writing !

HLEST. : I must own, I simply live for literature ! My house is the best known in Petersburg. Everybody knows it, they point it out to strangers. " That's Ivan Alexandrovitch's house." (*turns and addresses all present*) If you are ever in Petersburg, gentlemen, I hope you'll honour me with a visit. I give balls too.

ANNA : Oh ! I can imagine what they must be like !

HLEST. : You've no conception ! Now, for instance, I might have on the table, . . . a . . . a . . . a water-melon that cost me 700 roubles. (*gasps from the company*) And the soup I have brought on a fast steamer straight from Paris ! And the aroma as soon as you lift the lid ! Incomparable ! I go to balls every day ! When we're bored with dancing we may make up a four at whist, the Foreign Minister, the French Ambassador, the English Ambassador, the German Ambassador and I. But the ball ends at last, I go back to my little flat on the fourth floor, my cook comes, and I say, " My coat, Mavrushka ! " . . . (*stops and laughs unsteadily*) Oh ! But that's a good one ! Me living on the fourth floor ! Ivan Alexandrovitch, on the fourth floor ! Of course I live on the first floor. Why my staircase is worth . . . and if you looked into my hall in the morning, before I'm awake : princes and counts bustling and buzzing about like bees round a hive ! And ministers ! (*the Mayor and officials at this start nervously from their seats ; during the whole of this scene Hlestakov has been drinking glass after glass of wine from a tray on the table, and is now very drunk and in*

56

a highly-excited condition; he does not become inarticulate, or pronounce his "esses" as "sh"; the effect is shown by even greater gaiety and flights of fancy.) My letters all come addressed, "Your Excellency." I was once in charge of a department; it was very strange. The Director went away; he disappeared, and nobody knew where. And of course, there were the usual arguments, who was to succeed him? A lot of the generals wanted the job, and they took it on, one after the other, but they hadn't got enough there (*tapping forehead*). It looks easy, but when you go into it, . . . not so easy. So when they saw it was no use, they sent for me. Every minute! More messengers! Pouring along the street! You can imagine it! 35,000 messengers! What a state of affairs, I ask you! "Ivan Alexandrovitch, come and take charge of the department." I own, I felt a little uneasy. I felt like refusing, but I thought, well, it might come to the ears of the Tsar, and one has one's career to think of! "So be it!" I said, "I accept, gentlemen, but I—I—I— I have eyes in my head. You'd better look out, and if any of you try to . . ." And do you know, I went through that department like an earthquake, absolutely like an earthquake! Everything trembled and shook like a leaf! (*the Mayor and officials by now are trembling with fear, Hlestakov getting more worked up; his speech now is a little more jerky, and violent, but still clear.*) Oh! I'm not joking! I gave 'em all a regular tongue-lashing! I even put the fear of God into the Privy Council! Absolutely! I'm like that! I don't stop for anyone! I told them, "I know all about it! I see everything! I go everywhere!" I go to the Winter Palace every day! To-morrow I'm to be made a Field Marshal! (*during the last sentences he has been standing; he staggers once too often, slips, and nearly sprawls full length, but is caught and respectfully supported by the officials*).

MAYOR : (*shaking with fright from head to foot, can hardly speak*) Your . . . yo . . . you . . . your. . . .

HLEST. : (*quickly and abruptly*) What is it?

MAYOR : You . . . yo . . . your . . . ex . . .

HLEST. : (*in the same voice*) I can't make out what you're saying; it's nonsense.

57

MAYOR : Your . . . your ex . . . lency ! Wouldn't you like to lie down ? Your room is ready ; there's everything you need.

HLEST. : (*now standing, swaying very slightly*) Lie down ? Rubbish ! (*no one contradicts, so :*) All right. I don't mind lying down. That lunch of yours, gentlemen ! Excellent ! I am very pleased ! [*he draws himself up, and totters to the door of his room, gently guided by the Mayor, who opens the door for him. Hlest. turns in the door.*] Ladies ! Labardan ! Gentlemen ! Labardan ! [*He turns and goes through followed by the Mayor ; the audience is given a few seconds to photograph the attitudes and expressions of admiration, wonder, terror, and astonishment of those left on the scene, and as the door closes*]

THE CURTAIN FALLS.

ACT III SCENE 1

The same scene ; about 8 o'clock next morning.

[*the Mayor comes quietly on ; he is wearing a dressing gown over his breeches ; he goes to Hlestakov's door, listens, and is apparently satisfied that H. is deeply asleep ; he goes to the window, opens it, and calls quietly :*] Psst ! Hey ! Svistoonov and Dyerzhimorda ! come up here at once ! [*steps are heard and the two Constables enter, centre.*]

MAYOR : Shhh ! You clumsy bears ! Must you make a noise like a regiment on the march ? Where's Prohorov ?

CONST. : He's out with the watchmen cleaning the streets.

MAYOR : Oh ! He's sober, is he ? Now look, you, stand on those front steps and don't go wandering off for any reason whatever ! You hear ? And don't let anybody in at all, and certainly none of the tradespeople ! But if one of them does get in . . . you'll have to . . . Well, see that nobody gets in, with a petition or without a petition, or anybody who even looks as if he might want to bring a petition against me, throw them out head-first, you understand ! (*demonstrating a hearty kick*) Like that ! You hear ! (*his voice has risen, and realising it :*) Sh ! Shh ! See to it. [*the two Constables tip-toe off ; as they leave, Anna and Marya come on left, dressed up to the nines.*]

ANNA : Anton ! What are you doing here in that dressing gown ? You ought to be ashamed !

MAYOR : He's asleep. But don't make a noise ! My head's in a whirl. God knows what's going on inside it ! I feel as if I was going to be hung ! I couldn't sleep all night thinking of it !

ANNA : I didn't feel timid in his presence. I simply saw in him a well-born, cultured man of the world, and his rank didn't disconcert me.

MARYA : He's a darling !

ANNA : You can see he's a Petersburg dandy ! Such grace ! Such delicacy ! I took to him at once, and I noticed he kept stealing peeps at me !

MARYA : Now Mummy ! You know he was looking at me !

ANNA : Now God give me strength ! You're quite impossible ! We had all that out yesterday ! Why should he pay any attention to you ? Any more nonsense and I'll send you to your room !

MAYOR : Oh ! You women ! That one word's enough ! Always arguing ! I wish I knew how much of all that stuff he told us was true ! But why shouldn't it be ? When a man's in drink it all comes out. What's in the heart comes out of the mouth. He probably threw in a few fibs. Nothing is ever said without a few fibs. He plays cards with Ministers and

59

goes to the Palace every day ! It's his manner that's convincing !

ANNA : I shouldn't worry about it if I were you.

MAYOR : Oh ! It's no use talking to you ! (*musing to himself*) It is a queer business. I still haven't stopped shaking ! Wonderful how things have changed. Distinguished people ought to be something to look at, but this little whipper-snapper might be anybody ! How he kept it up at the inn, and concocted all those stories and taradiddles that a century wouldn't make sense of ! But he's given in at last, though he told us a good deal more than was necessary. It's obvious, he's a young hand.

[*Yosif enters softly from bedroom, shutting the door quietly behind him.*]

ANNA : Come here, friend.

MAYOR : Is your master asleep ?

YOSIF : Sound asleep.

ANNA : Listen. What's your name ?

YOSIF : Yosif, madam.

MAYOR : (*to his wife and daughter*) That will do, that will do. (*to Y.*) Now, friend, have you been well fed ?

YOSIF : Very well, thank you kindly.

ANNA : Tell me now, is your master visited by very many counts and princes ?

YOSIF : (*with peasant cunning*) Yes, ma'am, lots of them.

MARYA : Darling Yosif ! How handsome your master is !

ANNA : Tell me, Yosif, how he. . . .

MAYOR : That will do ! You're only hindering me with all these childish questions ! Now then, friend, what is your master like, stern ? Does he like finding fault ? Or is he easy to deal with ?

YOSIF : He likes things well run. Everything must always be just so !

ANNA : How does your master look in uniform ! What rank is he ?

MAYOR : God help us ! You and your insane curiosity ! You don't let me get in a word about important business. Now tell me, what kind of things does your master pay most attention to, on the road ? What does he like best ?

60

YOSIF : It all depends. Most of all he likes being well received and entertained.

ANNA : Listen Yosif ! What colour eyes does your master like best ?

MARYA : Darling Yosif ! What a dear little nose your master has !

MAYOR : Will you be quiet ! Insatiable chatterbox ! Can't you see it's important to find out what kind of man our guest is ? Now, friend, you were saying . . . what was it ?

YOSIF : Yes, he does like to be well entertained. Now here am I, his body servant, just a serf. But he always sees I'm well treated ! Oh, yes ! Often, when we've stopped at a place he asks me, " Have they looked after you well, Yosif ? " " No, very badly, your Honour." He says : " That's a bad place. Remind me when we reach home." And I think to myself, " God save him." I'm just a simple man.

MAYOR : Good, good. You know, I like your face. I can see you're a smart fellow. Now, an extra glass of tea comes in useful on the road nowadays . . . Here's a couple of roubles for you.

YOSIF : Thank you kindly, sir. God keep you in good health. You've helped a poor fellow.

MAYOR : I'm glad. Now then. . . .

ANNA : Well, I can't stay here chattering. I have things to do. I must see to the hospitality for our guest. Come and see me later, Yosif, I shan't forget you. (*Marya shows a wish to stay behind.*) Come along Mashenka, I have some things to tell you, that I have found out about our guest. We must have a talk. (*they go off, left.*)

MAYOR : What they won't talk about ! If you were to go and listen to them, your ears would blister ! Now, friend, I've taken quite a liking to you ; here's another rouble for biscuits.

[*enter the Charity Commissioner, the Postmaster, the School Superintendent, and the Judge, in full uniform, with swords, followed by Bobchinsky and Dobchinsky, dressed as before ; the Mayor greets them with a nod, and turns back to Yosif.*]

Go along, friend, and get things ready for your master. Ask for anything you need. [*Yosif goes into the bedroom.*] Well, gentlemen, this is an early hour for a call.

cc. : We came to pay our respects to His Excellency.

MAYOR : *(to Dob. and Bob.)* And you, Peter Ivanovitch?

DOB. : Oh! I have to see him about a most important matter! *(a faint grin on the Judge's face, and a cough from Artemy Filipovitch indicate that they have an idea what this matter is.)*

MAYOR : Have you done anything about your schools, Luka Lukitch?

ss. : What can one do? *(with a hopeless shrug)* It's the people!

MAYOR : Well, I must leave you, gentlemen. I must dress and see to a few little matters. I hope you have taken steps, and used the time well.

cc. : But you know, it's impossible to get rid of the smell in the hospital! It will take years!

MAYOR : *(sadly)* Yes, I know. *(a cough is heard from the bedroom.)*

[*the Mayor goes off hurriedly, left.*]

JUDGE : *(this scene is played* sotto voce) For goodness' sake, gentlemen, form a semicircle quickly. It looks better! God save us! He visits the Palace and terrifies the Privy Council! Stand in a rank, stand at attention! You Peter Ivanovitch, stand this end and you, Peter Ivanovitch, stand there! *(both Peter Ivanovitches, after some confusion, run round on tiptoe.)*

cc. : I don't know what you think, Ammos Fyodorovitch, but it seems to me we ought to do something.

JUDGE : Such as?

cc. : *You* know.

JUDGE : You mean . . .? *(gesticulates with hand behind back, suggesting bribery.)*

cc. : Yes! I thought we might . . .

JUDGE : No! Too dangerous! He might begin to bawl at us, a great man like that! But why not give it to him in the form of a subscription to some fund!

PM. : Or we could say, some money has been sent by post, and nobody knows who it belongs to!

cc. : Now listen: in a well-ordered country things are not done like that! Now why are we all here? Obviously, to introduce ourselves to him one by one, and then whatever happens is only seen by two pairs of eyes! That's how it's done in a well-ordered country! You'll go in first, of course, Ammos Fyodorovitch.

JUDGE : Much better if you went first. His Excellency has broken bread in your hospital.

CC. : Perhaps if Luka Lukitch went in first ; representing the enlightenment of youth!

SS. : No! I can't! I can't! It's the way I was brought up! Just to pass a remark with a man of higher rank makes my heart stop, and my tongue sticks in my throat! I'd much rather one of you went first.

CC. : You should go first Ammos Fyodorovitch. You've a gift of oratory as good as Cicero's.

JUDGE : What next? Cicero! Though I once made a very fine speech about dogs!

ALL : You're too modest! Don't fail us Ammos Fyodorovitch! Be our leader! (*coughing and footsteps are heard in Hlestakov's room ; everybody rushes to the centre doors, to see who can get out first ; there is a crush in the door, and yelps as somebody gets squeezed.*)

BOB : Ooh! Peter Ivanovitch! Somebody's treading on my toe!

CC. : Ooh! You're squashing me! Let go!

[*enter Hlestakov, rubbing the sleep out of his eyes, and Yosif.*]

HLEST. : Eeh! I must have been snoring beautifully! Where do they get such feather-beds? I'm still sweating like a bull. They must have given me something special at that lunch yesterday! My head is still drumming. (*pause*) You know, Yosif, I can have a very pleasant time here. I do like hospitable people, and I like it much better if they try to please me out of pure kindness, and not from self-interest.

YOSIF : They treat us very well. They were all asking me this morning what kind of things you liked. It's very strange. I don't understand it all.

HLEST. : You couldn't be expected to understand it. These people have never seen anybody of importance. But at least they are kind-hearted and know what is necessary. And the daughter is quite good looking, and I think the mother is ready for anything. I don't know why, but I like this kind of life.

[*enter Judge, very nervous. Yosif retires at a sign from Hlesta-kov.*]

JUDGE : I have the honour to introduce myself; Judge of the District Court, Collegiate Assessor, Lyapkin-Tyapkin. (*he has money clenched in his right fist.*)

HLEST. : Please sit down. So you are the judge here. Is the post profitable ? (*this throws the Judge into fresh terror, as he reads hidden meanings into it.*)

JUDGE : Well, after three terms I was honoured with the Order of St. Vladimir, of the 4th degree, and the authorities ap-proved of my work. (*aside :*) The money is in my fist, and my fist is on fire ! (*he holds this hand a little forward.*)

HLEST. : Yes, I like the Vladimir. The St. Anne is not nearly so nice. What's that you've got in your hand ?

JUDGE : (*panics and drops the notes on the floor*) Nothing !

HLEST. : Nothing ? I see you've dropped some money. (*picking it up*) It is money.

JUDGE : (*in extreme terror*) Oh no ! Oh yes ! Certainly ! Take it, Your Excellency, take it ! (*aside :*) I feel as if I were on trial for my life !

HLEST. : I'll tell you what. Let me have it as a loan. I got cleaned out on the road, you know. I'll send it to you when I reach my estate.

JUDGE : Please don't think of it. It is such an honour ! Really ! I endeavour to serve the authorities to the utmost of my poor powers ! My zeal ! My ardour for service, I . . . I . . . I shall do my best to deserve. . . . (*rising from chair, holds sword, standing at attention*) I shall not venture to trouble you further with my presence. Has Your Excellency any instructions for me ?

HLEST. : What kind of instructions ?

JUDGE : Am I to understand you have no special orders for my court ?

HLEST. : Why, no, I do not think there is any need just now, thank you.

JUDGE : (*bowing himself out, somehow finds the door ; aside :*) Well, the town is ours !

HLEST. : A good fellow ! The Judge !

64

[*Luka Lukitch, the School Superintendent, is shoved through the door; simultaneously we hear a remark,* sotto voce, *from the other side of it :*] What are you frightened about?

SS. : (*holding himself erect, sword in hand, not without considerable quaking.*) I have the honour to introduce myself ; School Superintendent, Titular Councillor, Hlopov.

HLEST. : Welcome ! Sit down ! Have a cigar ! (*the SS. is nonplussed and hesitant.*) Come, have one ! They're good cigars, though, of course, not what you'd get in Petersburg. When I'm in Petersburg, my cigars cost me 25 roubles a hundred ! Delicious ! (*kisses his hand and waves it theatrically.*) Like that ! Here, light it. (*brings candle from table.*) (*The SS. tries to light it, but, all nerves, takes the wrong end.*) That's the wrong end !

SS. : (*drops the cigar with fright, coughs and chokes ; aside :*) The devil take it ! My cursed timidity has ruined everything.

HLEST. : You don't seem to be a connoisseur of cigars. Now they're a weakness of mine. And, of course, the fair sex ! I can't resist them ! What about you ? Which do you prefer ? Blondes or brunettes ? (*the SS. is completely at a loss.*) Come now, you can be frank with me. Blondes or brunettes ?

SS. : I hardly venture to have an opinion.

HLEST. : Now, no excuses ! I should like to know your taste. (*the SS. is undecided, which to say.*) Ah ! You won't say ! I can see you're smitten on some pretty little brunette ! Now, confess ! You are ! (*no answer.*) Why ! You're blushing ! You see ! What did I say ?

SS. : I didn't like to, Your Hon. . . . Exc. . . . Beat . . . Excellency ! (*aside :*) Now my damned tongue's given me away !

HLEST. : (*charitably*) Yes, I know there is something about my eyes that puts fear into people ! I never found a woman who could resist them for long ! Eh ?

SS. : Quite so !

HLEST. : (*pauses a moment, looking sideways at Luka*) You know, a funny thing happened to me on the way here. I got completely cleaned out in a card game. Do you think you could lend me, say, 400 roubles ? I'll return it when I reach home.

ss. : God ! What if I haven't got it ? (*aloud :*) Yes, here it is. Don't dream of returning it Your Ex . . . Gra. . . . lency !

HLEST. : Thank you very much indeed.

ss. : (*draws himself up, holding sword*) I shall not venture to trouble you further with my presence. (*bows out.*)

HLEST. : Good bye ! Good bye !

ss. : (*almost running to door*) Thank God ! Perhaps he won't go into the schools now ?

HLEST. : (*laughing to himself, and luxuriating in his cigar*) He was terrified of me !

[*enter Zemlyanika, the Charity Commissioner.*]

cc. : I have the honour to introduce myself. (*drawing himself up, holding sword*) Commissioner for Charitable Institutions, Court Councillor, Zemlyanika.

HLEST. : Good morning, please sit down.

cc. : I had the privilege of conducting you round the Charitable Institutions.

HLEST. : Of course ! I remember. You gave us a very good lunch!

cc. : These things are a pleasure in the service of our country.

HLEST. : It's a weakness of mine, you know, good food. But tell me : it seems to me you were a little smaller yesterday !

cc. : That's not impossible. (*pause*) I can truly say that I am most zealous ; I never spare myself in the service. (*moves his chair up closer and speaks in an undertone*) And that's more than I can say for some people. Now the School Superintendent here . . . I don't know how the authorities can employ such a man ! He's worse than a Jacobin. He puts evil ideas into the minds of the young.

HLEST. : You don't say so !

cc. : And the judge, who came in here first, spends all his time coursing; his courthouse is full of dogs, and when I tell you about his conduct as I must though he's a friend and relation of mine . . ., his conduct is really scandalous. There is a landowner here, one Dobchinsky, that Your Excellency may have deigned to notice ; well, whenever this Dobchinsky leaves his house to go anywhere, the judge is immediately in with his wife, and I would swear . . . but look at the children, Your Excellency ! Not one of them is

66

like Dobchinsky, but every one, even the little girl, is the very image of the judge !

HLEST. : (*very amused*) Well, I should never have thought it of him !

CC. : And the Postmaster here does absolutely nothing ! His department is in chaos ; the mails are delayed for days ! If you wish, I can put all this better in writing.

HLEST. : Yes, yes. That will be very convenient. When I am alone, you know, I like to read something amusing. What is your name ? I have forgotten.

CC. : (*deliberately*) Artemy Filipovitch Zemlyanika.

HLEST. : And have you any children ?

CC. : Yes. Five. Two already grown up.

HLEST. : Grown up ! Eh ? And what are . . . what are their names ?

CC. : Nicolai, Iván, Elisavéta, Marya, and Perpetua.

HLEST. : Very nice.

CC. : (*erect, gripping sword*) I shall not venture to trouble you further with my presence, or to keep you from the tasks of duty. (*begins to bow out.*)

HLEST. : Oh, that doesn't matter. What you have been telling me is very interesting. Please come and see me again, I like that kind of thing. (*they have gone to the door, and just as Artemy is vanishing*) Oh, Artemy Filipovitch, would you do me a kindness ? A funny thing happened to me on the way here, I got absolutely cleaned out. Could you lend me, say, 400 roubles ?

CC. : Certainly. (*resignedly counts out the notes*).

HLEST. : Oh ! That's good, I'm very much obliged to you.

[*the CC. goes out. Dobchinsky and Bobchinsky hurry in, rather like moths drawn to the candle flame.*]

BOB. : I have the honour to introduce myself. Peter Ivanovitch Bobchinsky, a resident of the town.

DOB. : Peter Ivanovitch Dobchinsky, landowner.

HLEST. : Yes, I've seen you before (*to Bob.*) You, er, fell down at the inn. How's your nose ?

BOB. : Oh, please don't disturb yourself on my account. It's healed up now, thank God, quite healed up !

67

HLEST. : That's good, I'm very glad. (*sharply*) Have you any money with you?

DOB. : Money? What . . . ? Why?

HLEST. : A thousand roubles to lend me?

BOB. : Dear me! Not as much as that! You haven't either I suppose, Peter Ivanovitch?

DOB. : No, I haven't got it! (*to H.*) If you are pleased to be interested all my money has been lodged with the Public Trustee!

HLEST. : Well, if you haven't a thousand, I'll take a hundred.

BOB. : (*digging in pockets*) Have you a hundred, Peter Ivanovitch? I've only 40, and that's in notes.

DOB. : (*counting*) 25 roubles in all.

BOB. : Look again, Peter Ivanovitch. I know your right hand pocket has a hole in it; there may be money in the lining.

DOB. : No! There's nothing there.

HLEST. : Well, if you've only got 65 roubles, I can only have 65. (*taking notes and change.*)

DOB. : Might I take the liberty of begging your aid, in a most delicate matter?

HLEST. : Yes. What is it?

DOB. : It's a most delicate affair. You see, our eldest son was born before our marriage!

HLEST. : Yes?

DOB. : (*very embarrassed*) Well, that is, er, in a manner of speaking. Really he was born to us exactly as if it was in lawful wedlock, and then, of course, we tied the nuptial knots of holy matrimony! Yes! (*he is proud of this phrase*) but if you will be kind enough to see, I want him to be my son legally, and to bear my name, that is, er, Dobchinsky!

HLEST. : Very well. Let him bear your name. That's quite easy.

DOB. : I am sorry to have troubled you, but, you know, he's such a gifted boy! We have great hopes of him! He can say by heart all kinds of rhymes, and if he gets hold of a penknife, he can make you a little horse and cab, as quickly as any conjurer! Peter Ivanovitch can bear me out!

BOB. : Yes, he's a talented boy!

HLEST. : Good! Good! I shall certainly do my best. I'll speak about that, and I hope everything will be arranged. (*turning to Bob.*) And haven't you anything to tell me?

68

BOB. : I have a most humble request to make.

HLEST. : What about ?

BOB. : I beg of you, when you go back to Petersburg, say to all those great people that you know so intimately, senators and admirals and . . . say to them : " You know, Your Highness, or Your Excellency, as the case may be, in such-and-such a town lives one Peter Ivanovitch Bobchinsky." Just like that : " Lives one Peter Ivanovitch Bobchinsky."

HLEST. : Very well.

BOB. : And sometimes when you are in the Palace with our gracious Tsar, say to him : " Do you know, your Imperial Majesty, in such-and-such a town lives one Peter Ivanovitch Bobchinsky ? "

HLEST. : Very well.

DOB. : Pardon us for intruding upon you.

BOB. : Pardon us for intruding upon you.

HLEST. : Please don't apologise, it was a pleasure. [*the two go out.*] What a lot of officials there are here ! They seem to have taken me for somebody very important in the Government. What imbeciles ! I must have fooled them finely yesterday ! I must write and tell Tryapitchkin about this ; he writes articles, he could write a fine skit about it. Yosif ! Bring me some paper and ink. And when he starts in on anybody ! Look out ! He wouldn't spare his own father when it came to a jest, or money . . . he loves money. But they are good fellows, these officials. It's a point in their favour, lending me all this money. Let's see how much I've got. Four hundred from the judge, 400 from the school man, 400 from the health commissioner, Oho ! Over a thousand already, twelve hundred, and . . ! Now then captain ! If you were here now, we'd soon see who got the best of it !

[*enter Yosif with paper and ink.*]

HLEST. : Well ! You see, fool, how I'm received here ! They make a great fuss of me !

YOSIF : Yes, I do, glory be ! But do you know what, Ivan Alexandrovitch !

HLEST. : Eh ? (*begins to write.*)

YOSIF : Get away from here ! It's time we were gone !

HLEST. : Rubbish ! Why ?

YOSIF : You'd better. We've lingered on here two days . . . bless the people ! . . . But that's enough ! What's the good of staying about here ? You never know . . . somebody else may arrive . . . really Ivan Alexandrovitch ! And the horses here are fine ! We could be racing along !

HLEST. : No, I want to stay here a bit longer. It's a fine place. Perhaps to-morrow.

YOSIF : To-morrow ! Now's the time to be off ! They're making a great fuss over us now, but we ought to get away ! They've mistaken you for somebody else. Besides, your papa will be angry with you for dawdling so long on the way. We could be galloping away now, while there's the chance. They have capital horses here !

HLEST. : (*writing*) Take this letter to the post, and take my order for post-horses. See we get good horses, mind ! Tell the drivers I'll give them a rouble apiece to drive me like a special courier, and sing. (*continues writing*) Tryapitchkin will die with laughter !

YOSIF : I'll send it by the house-boy, and then I'll start packing up, so as to lose no time.

HLEST. : Very well, but bring me another candle.

YOSIF : (*goes out and speaks, off:*) Hey ! Listen, you ! There's a letter to go to the post. Tell the Postmaster it goes without a stamp, it's on Government service. And tell him to send round the very best horses, the express team. And say my master doesn't pay the fare. It's paid by Government. And tell him to look lively, or my master will be angry. Wait a minute, the letter isn't ready yet.

HLEST. : (*writing*) I wonder where he lives now ; on Post Office Street, or the Goróhovy ? He changes his rooms so often without paying the rent. I'll send it to Post Office Street, and chance it. (*signs and folds the letter ; Yosif brings the candle ; Hlestakov seals the letter ; the voice of the Constable on the steps is heard with a babble of voices.*)

CONST. : (*off*) Where are you shoving to, bushy-beard ? My orders are not to admit anybody.

HLEST. : (*gives letter to Yosif*) There you are, take it.

[the noise (off) increases; protesting voices are heard.]

VOICES OF SHOPKEEPERS : *(off)* Let us in ! Let us in ! You can't keep us out ! We have come on business !

CONSTABLE : *(off)* Go away ! Clear off ! He can't see you, he's asleep !

HLEST. : What's all that noise, Yosif ? Go and look.

YOSIF : *(at window)* It's some shopkeepers and people trying to get in, but the constable's stopping them ? They're waving pieces of paper ; they want to see you.

HLEST. : *(drawn to window)* What is it, friends ?

VOICES : We appeal to your gracious favour ! Tell them to accept our petitions, honoured sir !

HLEST. : Let them in ! Let them come in ! Yosif, go and tell him to let them in. *[Yosif goes off.] (Hlest. reaches through the window and takes a scroll:)* " To His Most Noble Highness, the Master of Finances, from the merchant Abdulin." Why ! The devil ! There's no such title !

[enter Yosif, and three merchants, one of them being Abdulin ; at least one should be a Jew ; all are bearded ; one is carrying a basket with wine and sugar-loaves ; they bow low.]

HLEST. : Well, friends ?

2ND MER. : We beg your favour, honoured sir !

HLEST. : *(rising to the occasion)* What do you want ?

3RD MER. : Do not ruin us ! We are suffering cruel wrong !

HLEST. : Who from ?

ABDULIN : From the Mayor. There never was a Mayor like him, never ! We can't find words for the things he does ! He's ruined us by billeting soldiers on us ; now there's nothing left to us but ropes round our necks and *(graphic gesture of slipping off a chair, hanging, etc.)* die ! His behaviour is not in reason. He pulls our beards and roars at us, " Ah ! You Tartar ! " As God's my witness ! If we had displeased him in any way, but we have always done what is expected : dresses for his wife and daughter, presents·at Easter, we don't mind that ! But that doesn't satisfy him !

HLEST. : Good Heavens ! He must be an absolute scoundrel !

2ND MER. : He comes storming down to the shop and takes anything he comes across ! If he sees a piece of cloth it's, " Ah !

My dear man ! Nice piece of cloth you've got there ! Send it round to my house ! " We have to send it, and it may be a 40-yard roll !

3RD MER. : We never had such a Mayor in living memory ! We have to hide everything in the shop when we see him coming. It isn't only the dainties he goes for ! He'll take any rubbish ! Plums that have lain seven years in the barrel, that my assistants wouldn't look at, he eats by the handful ! St. Anton's is his name-day, and then we take him all manner of things. But that isn't enough ! He says St. Basil's is his name-day, too, and we have to take him presents on that day too !

HLEST. : Why ! He's nothing but a brigand !

2ND MER. : He is ! But if you say a word, he'll billet a regiment on you. He'll shut up your business ! " I shan't have you flogged or tortured," he says, " that's forbidden by law ! But we'll feed you on salt herrings," he says, " till you feel a little thirsty."

HLEST. : What a villain ! They send people to Siberia for less than that !

3RD MER. : Wherever you're pleased to pack him off to . . . so long as it's a long way off. Do not scorn our simple offerings, good father, pray accept this sugar and wine, with our humble good wishes.

HLEST. : No ! Don't think of it ! I never take bribes ! But if you could offer me a loan, say, 300 roubles, that would be all right.

ABDULIN : By all means, honoured sir ! 300 roubles ! Why not five ? only rescue us ! (*the money is offered on a silver tray.*)

HLEST. : Very well ; I shall be happy to accept a loan.

2ND MER. : Please accept the tray with it.

HLEST. : Well, yes, I might take the tray also.

3RD MER. : And why not favour us by taking the sugar !

HLEST. : Oh, no ! I never take bribes !

YOSIF : But why not take it, Your Excellency ? It will all be useful on our journey. Give me the sugar and the basket, give me the whole lot ; it will all come in handy. What's that ? A piece of string ? String's useful on a journey, give me that too.

ABDULIN : Look kindly on our humble plea, Your Highness! If you will not help us, we have nowhere to turn to : there is nothing left to us but death.

HLEST. : Fear not! It will be done! [*the Merchants go out; a woman's voice is heard.*]

VOICE : (*off*) You daren't keep me out! I shall tell His Highness about you. Don't push me! It hurts!

HLEST. : Who's there? (*goes to window*) What is it, mother?

TWO FEMALE VOICES : (*off*) Save us! Help us! Grant us a hearing, good sir.

HLEST. : Let them in.

[*the locksmith's wife and sergeant's wife come in.*]

LOCK. : (*bowing to his feet*) I beg your help, good sir.

SERG. : (*bowing to his feet*) I beg your help, good sir.

HLEST. : But who are you? What is it?

SERG. : Ivánovna, wife of a sergeant.

LOCK. : Poshlyópkina, wife of the town locksmith.

HLEST. : Wait. Speak one at a time ; what is it?

LOCK. : It's the Mayor, good sir! Help me! God rot him, the scoundrel! Him, and his children and his uncle and his aunt, the plague o' the whole pack o' them! Curse them and everything they do!

HLEST. : What for?

LOCK. : He sent my man for a soldier, and it wasn't his turn ; it's against the law, to take a married man.

HLEST. : Then how can he do it?

LOCK. : Oh! he did it, he did it, all right! God blast him! In this world and the next! And the plague on his aunt, if he has one, and his father too! He ought to have taken the tailor's son, that drinks himself silly, but his parents persuaded (*bus. bribe*) him to let him go, then he picked on the draper woman's son, but she sent his wife three lengths of linen, so he came to us! " Your husband's a thief," he says, " but he's stolen nothing yet ; it's all the same, he'll steal one day," he says. " And here am I without a husband, a poor, weak woman," I said to him. " What do you want a husband for?" says he, " he's no use to you." Now I know best if my man's any use to me, that's my busi-

73

ness ; the swindler ! I said to him, " I hope all your grand-children die still-born, and your mother-in-law. . . ."

HLEST. : Yes, yes. That will do. (*turning to the other one*) Now, what's your complaint ?

LOCK. (*going out*) : You won't forget, sir ?

SERG. : It's the Mayor, sir ! He had me flogged, the nasty . . . !

HLEST. : Tell me briefly !

SERG. : By mistake, little father ! Some peasant women were fighting in the market, and the police came when it was all over, and reported me ! I couldn't sit down for two days !

HLEST. : But what can I do now !

SERG. : You can't take it back, but you could make him pay a fine ! The money would be very handy in these times . . .

HLEST. : Very well. You can go now. I shall see to it.

[*exit sergeant's wife; during the previous scene there have been occasional noises of a crowd (off) ; now this increases ; hands waving papers are seen through the window, and a few billets and scrolls are thrown into the room.*]

HLEST. : Who's that ? I don't want them. I don't want them. They mustn't do it ! I'm sick of them ! Tell them to go away.

YOSIF : (*shouting out of window*) Go away ! Clear off ! His Excellency will see no one now ! Come to-morrow. (*etc., ad lib.*)

[*while their attention is focused on the window, Hlest. standing concealed by the curtain, several figures enter by the centre door ; a man with unshaven face and swollen lip, bandaged over the cheek; others are seen through the door in a kind of perspective. Yosif turns from the window, pushing the foremost figure out and banging the door.*]

YOSIF : Go away ! Be off with you ! Where are you sneaking to ?

[*enter Marya Antonovna.*]

MARYA : (*seeing Hlestakov*) Oh !

HLEST. : What were you frightened of ?

MARYA : I wasn't frightened.

HLEST. : Forgive me ! I'm so pleased you aren't frightened of me. May I ask where you were going ?

MARYA : Really I wasn't going anywhere.

HLEST. : Why weren't you going anywhere ?

74

MARYA : I thought Mama was in here.

HLEST. : I should very much like to know why you weren't going anywhere.

MARYA : But I have disturbed you. You were occupied with your important business.

HLEST. : Your eyes are more important than any business. You could never disturb me, not anyhow. Your presence is solace to a weary heart ! Business ! Responsibilities ! In your presence they become less than nothing !

MARYA : Why ! You're talking the way they talk in high society !

HLEST. : To such an exquisite creature as you. May I give myself the happiness of offering you a chair ? But no ! For you it should be a throne !

MARYA : Really, I ought to be going. (*sits*.)

HLEST. : What a beautiful necklace you have on !

MARYA : You are just making fun of us poor provincials !

HLEST. : If only I could be that necklace, to embrace your lily-white neck !

MARYA : I don't quite understand what you are talking about. Isn't the weather strange to-day ?

HLEST. : Your cherry lips are more to me than any weather.

MARYA. : You do say such things ! Will you write some verses in my album ?

HLEST. : What kind of verses would you like ? I know so many. For you I would do anything.

MARYA : Will you write me some of your own ? Something . . . anything . . . clever, and new.

HLEST. : What about this ?* " To be or not to be, that is a question ! " (*emphasises "is"*) There are plenty of others, but at the moment, I can't remember them. Instead of verses I would much rather offer you my love which your beautiful eyes have poured into my heart. (*moves chair nearer.*)

MARYA : Love ? I don't quite understand about that. I'm never quite sure what it means. (*moves chair away.*)

HLEST. : (*moving nearer*) Why do you move your chair ? It would be nicer if we sat near each other.

---

* Hlestakov is not a well-read person. In the original at this point he quotes a completely irrelevant tag he happens to have remembered from his schooldays. " To be . . ," etc. is about the nearest equivalent, and it is funnier if he misquotes.

MARYA : (*moving away*) What for ? It makes no difference if we aren't so near.

HLEST. : (*moving nearer*) But why move. You must imagine to yourself that we are far apart. How happy it would make me if I could hold you in my arms ! (*kisses her on the shoulder.*)

MARYA : (*rising*) Now that's too much ! You think because I'm a country girl, that . . . (*tries to get away.*)

HLEST. : (*holding her*) Forgive me ! It was my love for you that made me do it ! Just my love ! Forgive me ! Marya Anton-ovna ! Don't be angry with me ! I'll go down on my knees . . . (*does so*) Forgive me ! You see I'm on my knees before you !

[*enter Anna Andreyevna.*]

ANNA : Oh ! What a scene ! (*Hlest. rises*) What does this mean, young madam ? What kind of behaviour is this ?

MARYA : Mummy ! I . . .

ANNA : Leave the room ! You hear ? And don't let me set eyes on you in here ! [*Marya goes out, in tears.*]

HLEST. : (*aside :*) She's very fetching too ; not bad at all. (*falling on his knee*) Madame, you see, I am burning with love !

ANNA : What ? On your knees ? Oh ! get up ! Please get up ! This floor is anything but clean !

HLEST. : No ! On my knees I beg of you, tell me my fate ! Is it life, or death ?

ANNA : Pardon me, I don't quite understand you ! If I am not mistaken, you are asking for my daughter's hand ?

HLEST. : No ! It is you I love ! My life is hanging by a thread ! If you will not requite my undying love, then, I am un-worthy to walk the earth ! With heart aglow, I beg your hand !

ANNA : But allow me to mention that I am, in a manner of speak-ing, married !

HLEST. : No matter ! What are mere formalities, beside an undying love ? We will fly to some shady dell by a crystal stream. I ask your hand !

[*Marya comes running in.*]

MARYA : Mummy, Daddy says you must . . . Oh ! What a scene !

ANNA : Now what is it ? Little Miss Flibberty-gibbet ! Dashing about like a scalded cat ! Nobody would ever imagine you were eighteen ! You behave like a child of three ! I can't imagine when you'll learn how a well-bred young girl should behave ! Such disgraceful manners ! What will His Excellency think of you ?

MARYA : (*dissolving in tears*) I'm sorry, Mummy. I didn't think . . .

ANNA : Such a scatter-brain ! One would think your head was filled with wind ! You're just like the Lyapkin-Tyapkin girl. And you've plenty of better people to imitate ! Your mother, for one !

HLEST. : (*taking Marya by the hand*) Anna Andreyevna, do not spoil our happiness ! Give a mother's blessing on our eternal love !

ANNA : (*dumbfounded*) Oh ! So it's her, after all ?

HLEST. : Speak ! Is it life or death ?

ANNA : There now ! You see, you little silly, his Excellency was on his knees to me, just for your sake ! And you come rushing in like a mad thing ! It would serve you right if I refused !

MARYA : I won't do it again, Mummy, really I won't.

[*enter the Mayor, breathless.*]

MAYOR : Your Excellency ! Spare me ! Spare me !

HLEST. : What's the matter with you ?

MAYOR : Those shopkeepers have been complaining to you. I give you my word of honour, not half of it's true ! They're such liars, always cheating people ! They're famous for giving short measure ! That sergeant's wife told you a lot of lies, if she said I flogged her ! She flogged herself !

HLEST. : The devil take the sergeant's wife ! What do I care !

MAYOR : Don't believe it ! Don't believe it ! They're such liars, they wouldn't deceive a child ! All the town knows it ! There isn't such a pack of heartless villains anywhere on earth !

ANNA : Do you know the honour Ivan Alexandrovitch is doing us ? He has asked our daughter's hand in marriage !

MAYOR : What next ? You must be raving mad ! Don't be angry, Your Excellency, she never was very strong in the head. Her mother was the same !

77

HLEST. : But really, I ask your daughter's hand ! I love her.

MAYOR : I can't believe it, your Excellency !

ANNA : But he's told you so !

MAYOR : I can't believe it ! Your Excellency is pleased to joke !

HLEST. : If you refuse me your daughter's hand, God knows what I might not do !

ANNA : What a blockhead you are ! Isn't he telling you himself ?

HLEST. : Consent ! Consent ! I am a desperate man ! If I should shoot myself, you will be to blame ! But perhaps you do not want me as a son ! You want to refuse politely ! Then there is nothing left but to end my useless life !

MAYOR : Oh, good heavens, no ! I never was guilty of that, in mind or heart. Let it be as Your Excellency wishes. My head ! I don't know what . . . it's going round and round ! I feel the biggest fool.

ANNA : Now give them your blessing ! (*the couple join hands in front of him, and he gives a father's blessing.*)

MAYOR : May God bless you. I'm not to blame, really. (*Hlest. embraces Marya, the Mayor looking on, still nonplussed.*) Well, now ! They're kissing each other, embracing ! (*rubs his eyes and stares*) Good Heavens ! They're kissing ! They're in love ! What a fine son-in-law ! (*he is jumping for joy*) Hey ! Anton ! Hey ! Anton ! Cheers for the Mayor ! (*sobered*) What a change in things !

[enter Yosif.]

YOSIF : The horses are ready.

HLEST. : Right. I'll be there in a minute.

MAYOR : But wha . . . ? What ? Is Your Excellency leaving us ?

HLEST. : Yes. I must go.

MAYOR : But when shall we . . . I mean, you were pleased to say something a moment ago, about marriage, wasn't it ?

HLEST. : Er, yes, but you see I must go away for a minute, that is, for a day, to see my uncle ; he's a rich old man. I must ask his blessing. I'll be back to-morrow.

MAYOR : We should not venture to keep you . . . we shall look forward to your return.

HLEST. : Of course ! I'll be back soon. Goodbye, my love ! Goodbye, my darling ! (*kisses her hand.*)

MAYOR : Won't you need anything for the road? I believe Your Excellency was a little short of money?

HLEST. : Oh no! (*considers*) Well, yes, perhaps.

MAYOR : How much would you like?

HLEST. : Well, you lent me 200, I mean 400—I don't want to take advantage of your mistake! If you could let me have the same again, that would make a round 800.

MAYOR : Certainly! There, brand new notes, as if I'd known!

HLEST. : (*counts notes and stows them away*) Thank you. You know they say, " New notes, new happiness."

MAYOR : Yes, indeed.

HLEST. : Goodbye, Anton Antonovitch! Delighted with your hospitality! I say this with feeling : I never was so well entertained in my life! [*they go out; the scene till curtain-fall is played off-stage*]. Goodbye Anna Andreyevna! Goodbye! My darling Marya Antonovna! Goodbye! Angel of my heart!

MAYOR : What's this? Are you going in the ordinary public chaise?

HLEST. : Yes, I prefer it; springs make my head ache.

MAYOR : Well, at least have something to sit on! Hey! Avdotya! Go and get that Persian rug with the blue ground! Quickly!

DRIVER : Whoaah!

MAYOR : When are we to expect Your Excellency?

HLEST. : To-morrow or the day after.

YOSIF : That the rug? Give it here! The straw that side!

DRIVER : Whoaah! My beauties!

YOSIF : No, over here with the straw! That's good! Now, will Your Honour be seated?

HLEST. : Goodbye, Anton Antonovitch!

MAYOR : Goodbye, your Excellency!

ANNA and MARYA : Goodbye, Ivan Alexandrovitch!

DRIVER : Hey! My beauties! My fliers!

(*the troika bells tinkle, sounds of two horses galloping, one trotting.*)

THE CURTAIN FALLS.

ACT III SCENE 2

The scene is the same: the time, later on the same day; the Mayor, his wife and daughter, are on at curtain-rise.

MAYOR : Well, Anna, did you ever imagine this might happen ? What a fine match ! Now admit it frankly, you never thought in your wildest dreams, that from being just a Mayor's wife, suddenly . . . I mean, dash it . . . to be allied with such a fine young devil !

ANNA : Not at all. I knew it all along. Of course, it's marvellous to you, because you're a simple fellow. You've never mixed with decent people.

MAYOR : Now, Mother, I'm not so bad myself. But do you realise, Anna, we've become birds of a different feather now ! Why bless my soul, we shall fly high ! Now I shall make it hot for all those fellows who came running round with complaints and petitions ! (*goes to door and calls*) Hey ! You there ! (*enter Svistoonov.*) Ah ! It's you, Ivan Kárpovitch ! Fetch all the shopkeepers here, friend ! Complain about me, would they ? Ungrateful dogs ! (*addressing them in imagination*) Wait ! My pretty dears ! Dirty Jew-dogs ! It'll be much worse for you now ! (*to Constable*) Take a list of all the people who came whining about me, and specially, the scribblers who wrote their petitions. And tell everybody the news, see they all know that God has seen fit to honour their Mayor ; that I'm giving my daughter in marriage, not to any country clod, but to a great dignitary from Petersburg, a paragon, a man who can accomplish anything, anything ! Tell them all, shout it in the market-place ! Let everybody know it ! Ring the bells, damn it ! If you're going to celebrate, then celebrate, I say ! [*exit*

Svistoonov.] That's that! Now all this has happened, my dear, where shall we live? Here or in Petersburg?

ANNA : In Petersburg of course, why should we stay here?

MAYOR : Mmmmm . . . if we live in Petersburg we live in Petersburg. Though I quite like it here. But of course, the Mayoralty can go to the devil!

ANNA : I should think so! Being a country Mayor!

MAYOR : And besides, you know, I may get a better rank now! He knows all the Ministers intimately and goes to court every day, and if they can give a poet such high promotion, who knows? With time I might be a general? Anna, do you think I might be made a general?

ANNA : Of course, Anton!

MAYOR : The devil! It would be fine to be a general! And wear orders and a sash over one's shoulder! Which ribbon do you like best Anna? The red or the blue?

ANNA : Obviously the blue is the prettiest!

MAYOR : You covet the blue one? Well, the red is handsome too! There's something about being a general! If you happen to travel anywhere, adjutants and orderlies gallop ahead to call for horses; and when you reach the posting stations, nobody else gets a look in, they all have to wait until the general is attended to! Mixing with all the councillors and captains, and not turning a hair! You may dine somewhere at the Governor's and there, he . . . he . . . he! Some poor wretch of a mayor has to stand while you sit in comfort! (*explodes with laughter at this exquisite joke*) It must be grand to be a general!

ANNA : Such coarse ways you have! You must remember, life will be quite different! You'll have different friends! No common judges stinking of dogs, that you go poisoning hares with, or that dirty Zemlyanika! Your friends will be members of the highest society, counts and men about town! But I'm worried about you! You use the most dreadful expressions, that one never hears in good company!

MAYOR : What about it? No harm in words.

ANNA : Of course it didn't matter what you said, when you were a mere Mayor. But there life will be different.

MARYA : (*who is accustomed to being ignored by her parents, but thinks this day might be an exception*) But Mummy ! What will happen when I'm married ?

ANNA : Hush child ! You shouldn't be bothering your head with such things, your father and I will see to everything !

MARYA : But it's me he is going to marry . . .

ANNA : Such ideas ! Well, perhaps it is you he is marrying, but you have your mother to thank for that. We shall be with you. I think I shall make our house the smartest in Petersburg ! I shall have scent in my boudoir so strong it will make everyone screw up their eyes when they come in ! (*screws up her eyes and sniffs vigorously*) Mmmmm ! Delicious !

[*shuffling noises (off); enter the Merchants as in Act III Sc. 1.*]

ALL MERS. (*bowing low*) : We wish you good health, sir !

MAYOR : (*sweeter than honey at first, then like a suppressed volcano which finally erupts*) Thank you, my friends. And how's business ? How are you to-day ? Well ? My pretty doves ? My falcons ? You don't like me, eh ? You cheap jacks ! You cloth-stretchers ! You tea-swillers ! You offal-merchants ! Complain about me, would you ? You good-for-nothing, gutterscraping, counter-jumpers ! Thought you'd get me put in prison, did you ? By the witch and the seven devils, I . . . !

ANNA : Anton ! What language !

MAYOR : Oh, don't fuss now ! Do you know, that that Inspector you ran whining to, is going to marry my daughter ? What do you say to that ? (*to 2nd Mer.*) You make a 100,000 on a government contract by supplying rotten cloth, give me 20 yards and expect a reward for it ! And the way he sticks his belly out ! You're a merchant, my man ! Not an armchair ! (*to 3rd Mer.*) And I've heard of your braggings ! So we count ourselves as good as a nobleman, do we ? You pig ! A nobleman learns manners ! If they beat him when he's at school it's to teach him knowledge ! But you . . . the master would beat you to teach you how to cheat ! When you were a small boy you knew how to give short measure before you learned your " Our Father." And the bigger your belly gets the more airs you put on! What a prodigy! Because you empty sixteen samovars a day you think you're a nobleman! Well, I don't give a fig for your nobility or you either!

3RD MER. : *(bowing)* We are to blame, Anton Antonovitch!

MAYOR : *(to Abdulin)* And who showed you how to make a fortune on that bridge contract when you put the timber down at 20,000 roubles and it wasn't worth a hundred! I helped you, goat-beard! And I can also send you to Siberia! What about that?

ABDULIN : The devil tempted us. We're very sorry we complained! We'll do the right thing for you, but don't be angry!

MAYOR : It's " Don't be angry " now, is it? Why are you crawling to me? Because I've got the whip hand! If you had it, you pigs, you'd trample me in the mud and batter me with a log!

2ND MER. : Don't ruin us, Anton Antonovitch!

MAYOR : " Don't ruin us! " What was it before? *(with the air of a deeply wronged man)* Well, God pardons all! I don't bear malice. But see it doesn't happen again. I'm marrying my daughter soon, but not to any petty landowner! Congratulations are in order, you understand! And they'd better be substantial! None of your dried fish and sugar-loaves! Well, God be wi' you!

[*exeunt Merchants ; enter the Judge and his wife, then the Charity Commissioner.*]

JUDGE : Are these rumours true, Anton Antonovitch? Has this extraordinary piece of luck come your way?

CC. : I have the honour to congratulate you on your great good fortune. When I heard it, I was delighted. *(crosses to Anna and Marya)* Anna Andreyevna! *(kisses her hand.)* Marya Antonovna! *(kisses her hand.)*

[*enter Rastakovsky.*]

RASTAKOVSKY : Congratulations, Anton Antonovitch! May God give you and the happy pair long life and numerous progeny! Grandchildren and great-grandchildren! *(crosses to women, kissing hands)* Anna Andreyevna! Marya Antonovna!

[enter Korobkin and his wife.]

KOROB. : I have the honour to congratulate you, Anton Antonovitch ! *(crosses to women, same bus. of names and kissing hands.)*
WIFE : I do congratulate you, Anna, on your new good fortune !

[a number of guests enter, cross, kiss hands and stand round.]
[enter Dobchinsky and Bobchinsky, bustling.]

BOB. : I have the honour to congratulate you !
DOB. : Anton Antonovitch ! I have the honour to congratulate
you ! A most propitious occasion !
BOB. : Anna Andreyevna !
DOB. : Anna Andreyevna ! *(they both try to kiss her hand at the
same time, and their heads collide.)* Marya Antonovna ! I have
the honour to congratulate you ! You will be a great, great
lady now, and wear dresses of gold ! You will eat the most
rare and delicate dishes and pass your time most amusingly !
BOB. : Marya Antonovna, I have the honour to congratulate
you ! May God give you great riches, yes ! A sack of gold
and a baby boy little enough to sit in your hand ! *(showing
with hand)* He'll be a fine boy with good lungs, Wah !
Wah ! Wah ! *(imitates baby crying.)*

[enter the School Superintendent and wife, and more guests.]

SS. : I have the honour . . .
WIFE : *(hurries to Anna.)* I congratulate you Anna ! *(they kiss.)*
I'm very glad ! They told me : Anton Antonovitch's
daughter is being married ! " Merciful heavens," I thought
to myself ! I said to my husband, " Listen, Lukanchik,
Anna Andreyevna has been so lucky ! I'm so delighted.
I'm all impatient to congratulate her myself. She certainly
expected a good match for her daughter and it's just the
workings of fate," I said, I was so delighted I could hardly
speak, I was crying for joy ! Simply sobbing ! Then Luka
Lukitch said, " What are you crying for ? " " I really don't
know," I said, " The tears just come in floods ! "
MAYOR : I beg you to be seated, ladies and gentlemen ! Mishka !
Bring more chairs ! *(all sit.)* *[enter the Police Superintendent.]*

PS. : (*to Mayor*) I have the privilege of congratulating Your Honour, and to wish you long life and prosperity.

MAYOR : Thank you, thank you.

JUDGE : Tell us how it began Anton Antonovitch ; tell us about the whole affair.

MAYOR : It was extraordinary ! He was kind enough to make the proposal in his own person.

ANNA : In the most charming and delicate manner. He did it beautifully ! He said to me : " Anna Andreyevna, your virtues hold me in thrall ! "

MARYA : But Mummy. . . .

ANNA : Be quiet, child ! He's such a splendid well-bred, gentleman, of the noblest principles ! He said so sincerely, " Believe me, Anna Andreyevna, life is nothing to me. I value it only because it has shown me your rare qualities."

MARYA : But Mummy, he said that to me !

ANNA : Nonsense, child, you know nothing about it ! He spoke the most flattering, passionate words. I felt like saying, " I never dared to hope for such honour," and finally he fell on his knees and said in the most charming way, " Anna Andreyevna, if you cannot feel for me, as I do for you, I must end my life ; I must kill myself."

MARYA : But Mummy, how can you ? He said that about me !

ANNA : There, there ! It may have been about you, I don't deny it !

MAYOR : I was terrified, I can tell you ! The way he kept on saying " I shall shoot myself, I shall shoot myself ! "

SS. : Go on ! Tell us the rest !

MAYOR : Well, it was just destiny !

CC. : Not destiny. It was the reward of industry and merit ! (*aside :*) Trust a pig to smell out the rich feeding !

KOROBKIN'S WIFE : You can't think how happy I am about your good fortune, Anna !

KOROB. : But allow me to ask, where is our distinguished guest ?

MAYOR : He has left us for a day or two, on very important business.

ANNA : To see his uncle, and get his blessing on the match.

MAYOR : Yes, to get his blessing, but to-morrow (*he sneezes; there is a hum of compliments.*) Thank you very much ; he'll be back to-morrow . . . (*sneezes again; another buzz of compliments, loudest of which are :*)

PS. : Good health to Your Honour.

BOB. : A hundred years of life and a sack of gold !

JUDGE'S WIFE : The devil take you !

CC. : The plague on you !

MAYOR : Many thanks. I wish you the same.

ANNA : We intend to live in Petersburg now. Here, I must say, it's a little too rustic ! My husband here . . . (*shrugs her shoulders*) but of course, he will be a general in Petersburg !

MAYOR : Yes, friends, I must own, I should very much like to be a general !

SS. : And God grant you succeed.

RAST. : Everything is possible with God.

JUDGE : A great ship must sail in deep waters.

CC. : Yes, merit will get its reward.

JUDGE : (*aside :*) A fine trick, if he is made a general ! It would be as suitable as a saddle on a cow ! But he's got a long way to go ! There are better men than he in this room who aren't generals.

CC. : (*aside :*) I'm afraid he will be made a general ; he's behaving like one already. (*to Mayor*) But you mustn't forget your old colleagues, Anton Antonovitch.

JUDGE : And you'll grant us your patronage in case we need any help, if anything went wrong, for example !

KOROB. : I shall be bringing my son to the capital next year, to enter him in the Service. I hope you'll do me the favour of taking him under your protection, and keeping a fatherly eye on him.

MAYOR : I shall be very happy to do what I can.

ANNA : Yes, Antosha, you're always ready to promise anything. In the first place, you won't have time for things like that. And if you had why burden yourself with a lot of promises ?

MAYOR : Why, my dear. Sometimes one can find time for a good turn.

ANNA : Oh, I know ! But must you promise your patronage to every nobody ?

KOROB.'S WIFE : Oh ! You hear what she thinks of us !

GUESTS : (*ad lib.*) Yes, she was always like that. I know her. It doesn't take much to unbalance her. Sit her at a table ; she'll put her feet on it !

[*enter Postmaster.*]

POSTM. : (*he is nervous and distraught, comes in waving a letter*) Ladies and gentlemen, something terrible has happened !

MAYOR : Well ? What is it ? We are all listening.

POSTM. : I can't . . . I really don't know what to say ! It's so unexpected ! We never dreamed. . . .

GUESTS : Well ? What is it ? Tell us !

POSTM. : (*looks round wildly, realises he will be torn in pieces if he explodes the news straightway; takes a deep breath, gulps, and commences a roundabout explanation*) I was just going home when I happened on a letter from that official we showed round. It was addressed to Tryapitchkin, Post Office Street, St. Petersburg. And when I read the words : " Post Office Street," I was thunderstruck ! That's a report about me, I thought. Well, it may be that I have, upon occasion gone so far, now and then, as to open letters for my own amusement. And as I stood there I could feel some invisible power compelling me to open the letter.

JUDGE : What ? His own letter ?

MAYOR : You mean to say . . . ? (*general horror.*)

POSTM. : (*hastily*) Of course I was horrified at the idea, and I left the letter on the table, meaning to send for the postillion to take it out quickly to the bag. But if I took one step away from that table, something dragged me back ! A voice cried in one ear, " Don't open it," and another voice said, " Open it ! Open it ! " One voice said, " Don't open it ! It will be your ruin if you do ! " The other voice said, " Open it, you fool ! It will be your ruin if you don't ! " My hands felt as if some huge magnet was pulling . . . ! I stood there ten minutes undecided ; finally I opened it !

MAYOR : How dared you open it ?

POSTM. : Well, so help me God, I opened it ! I've never been so terrified in my life ! I shut the shutters, locked the door, blocked the keyhole, and broke the seals with my own hand ! And when I touched the wax, fire ran in my veins, my body felt on fire ! And when I unsealed it, frost surged over me !

I was racked with icy shiverings ! Fire and ice ! My head
swam ! I didn't know where I was ! My teeth chattered so,
for a whole hour I couldn't read a line !

MAYOR : But how dared you open the mail of such an important
personage ?

POSTM. : But that's just it ! He isn't important and he isn't a
personage. He wasn't the Inspector-General !

MAYOR : (*unperturbed and urbane, quelling the others' questions with a
hand*) Well, since you know so much, what is he ?

POSTM. : Neither one thing nor the other ! The devil only knows
who he is !

MAYOR : What do you mean ? How dare you speak of him like
that ? I arrest you ?

POSTM. : Who ? You ?

MAYOR : Yes ! Me !

POSTM. : You couldn't if you tried !

MAYOR : Do you know he's going to marry my daughter? I shall be
a Petersburg grandee then, and I'll have you sent to Siberia!

POSTM. : (*nervously*) Eeh ! Siberia ! It's a long way off, you know,
Siberia ! But I'd better read you the letter. May I ?

ALL : Read it ! Read it !

POSTM. : " My dear Tryapitchkin : I must write and tell you about
my marvellous adventures lately. I told you how I got
cleaned out by an infantry captain in Penza ; well, I finally
got stranded here. The innkeeper fellow wanted to send
me to jail. I didn't write to the old man ; he's furious with
me, told me never to ask him for another copek. Well,
suddenly, owing I suppose to my Petersburg clothes and
distinguished looking face, the whole of this damned town
took me for the Governor-General ! And now I'm living
in the Mayor's house, having the time of my life, and
carrying on desperate flirtations with his wife and daughter.
My only trouble is, I can't decide which to go for first !
I think, the old lady ; she seems to be ready for anything !
Do you remember when we were both hard up, and the
pastry-cook threw me out of the shop for putting down my
pies to the King of England ? Well, it's quite different now !
Everybody presses money into my hand, always as loans,
of course ! Frightful half-wits ! You'd die laughing ! First

there's the Mayor : he's a generous chap, his hospitality is like a pole-axe, but he's as stupid as an old grey mule!"

MAYOR : That's not true! You're making it up as you go along!

POSTM. : Very well! Read it yourself!

MAYOR : " As an old grey mule." Impossible! You wrote this yourself!

POSTM. : How could I write such a letter?

CC. and SS. : Read it! Read it!

POSTM. : " As an old grey mule . . ."

MAYOR : Devil take you! Do you have to go on saying it? As if it wasn't bad enough?

POSTM. : Mmmmm. " As an old grey mule. The Postmaster is a good fellow. He . . ." Mmmmmmm. That's only rude remarks about me.

MAYOR : Go on, read it!

POSTM. : Why?

MAYOR : If you're going to read it, then read it all!

CC. : Give it to me. (*puts on spectacles.*) " The Postmaster looks and smells exactly like our hall-porter, Mikhéyev ; the one that drinks methylated spirits! "

POSTM. : He's just a wretched boy who needs a good whipping! That's all!

CC. : " The Charity Commissioner. . ." Mmmmmm.

KOROB. : What's the matter?

CC. : It's illegible just here. (*sotto voce :*) The rascal!

KOROB : (*with intent*) Give it to me. I have better eyes than you!

CC. : No, it gets better after a few lines.

KOROB. : Yes, I know. Give it to me!

CC. : No, I can read it. It gets legible further on.

POSTM. : No, you don't! Read every word! Give it up! (*rest ad lib.*)

CC. : Very well. (*to Korob. pointing with finger*) Look that's where I got to ; read from there.

ALL : (*ad lib., expressing exasperation with his obvious subterfuges.*)

KOROB. : " The Charity Commissioner, Zemlyanika, looks exactly like a sow in a nightcap."

CC. : That's not even funny! What would a sow be doing in a nightcap?

KOROB. : " The School Superintendent reeks of garlic from every pore." (*the reaction to this makes it obvious that it is true ; the name " Luka " means garlic.*)

SS. : Dear me ! I never ate garlic in my life !

JUDGE : Thank God, there's nothing so far about me !

KOROB. : " The Judge " . . .

JUDGE : Ladies and gentlemen, this letter is too long ! Only a madman would write such drivel !

SS. : Oh no ! Read it all ! (*CC., Postmaster, ad lib.*)

KOROB. : " The Judge is extremely (*hesitates, mispronounces it*), mauvais ton " . . . that must be a French word . . .

JUDGE : It might mean anything. I don't mind if it only means scoundrel, but it might mean something much worse !

KOROB. : " Otherwise, they are generous, hospitable people. Goodbye, my dear Tryapitchkin. I am trying to follow your example and devote my life to literature. Life is so dull, one must have food for the mind. I realise now that every man must pursue high ideals. Write to me at the village of Podkatílovka, province of Saratov." (*turns letter over and reads address*) It is addressed to Ivan Vassilyevitch Tryapitchkin, No. 97, top floor, on the right, turning left through the courtyard, Post Office Street, St. Petersburg.

SS.'S WIFE : What an unexpected blow !

MAYOR : This is killing ! The murderer ! He's stabbed me ! It's my death blow ! I can see nothing ! I can only see pig's snouts, instead of faces, nothing more ! Fetch him back ! Fetch him back ! (*waves wildly.*)

POSTM. : How ? I told the overseer to give him the very best team. And the devil made me give him a priority warrant !

KOROB.'S WIFE : What a dreadful blow ! I never remember anything so upsetting !

JUDGE : Good God ! And I gave him 400 roubles !

CC. : So did I !

SS. : He got 400 out of me too !

BOB. : And Peter Ivanovitch and I gave him 65 roubles between us !

JUDGE : (*spreading out his hands in resignation*) Well, friends, we just made a mistake, that's all !

MAYOR : (*who has been fuming steadily since the letter was read, clutching his head*) How could I, how could I ? I-I-I've been a fool !

After thirty years in the service . . . ! I've never been taken in in my life ! Not a tradesman, not a contractor has ever got the better of me, never ! I've swindled the swindlers by the thousand ! Rogues and rascals, that would have stolen the whole world, I've tripped 'em all up ! I've hoodwinked three governors ! Not that governors are anything much.

ANNA : But this can't be true, Antosha ! Why, he is engaged to Mashenka !

MAYOR : Engaged ! Engaged ! Even you throw it at me ! Look ! Just look ! All the world, all Christianity, everybody ! Look what a fool I've been ! (*to himself, threatening to hit himself with his fist*) You dolt ! You blockhead ! You imbecile ! You fat nose ! To take that milksop, that nincompoop, for a man of importance ! I can think of nothing but that damned scoundrel flying along the road with his troika bells ringing ! He'll tell everybody in Russia about it ! It's not enough that I shall be a laughing stock. Some jackanapes will write a play about it ! Some half-starved scurrilous scribbler ! Oh ! He'll lay it on ! My rank ! My experience ! My grey hairs ! No mercy ! The idiots will grin, and clap . . . ! What are you laughing at ? You are laughing at yourselves ! (*these lines, addressed to his imaginary audience, are the most famous in the play; in Russia they are usually spoken to the real audience.*) (*stamps his feet on the floor in desperation, yet is not without some shreds of forlorn dignity; is silent for a moment.*) All these inkslingers ! Pen scratchers ! Cursed liberals ! If I had 'em, I'd grind them to pulp ! (*demonstrates with heel.*) I still can't come to my senses ! They say that when God means to punish a man, he begins by taking his wits away. But what first put this chatter about an Inspector General into my brain ? Nothing ! Did that straw, that broomstick, look like one ? But all of a sudden everybody began buzzing : " The Inspector." " The Inspector's here." Now who was it made out that he was the Inspector-General ? Tell me that ! (*Bob. and Dob. have begun looking at each other in terror.*)

CC. : I couldn't tell you, if you killed me !

SS. : (*as one remembering dead centuries*) There was a letter . . .

JUDGE : Yes ! That morning . . . you sent for us. . . .

MAYOR : (*snorts*.) Yes, yes ! But who said *he* was the Inspector-General ?

JUDGE : Yes, now . . . Who was it ? I know ! Those two fine fellows ! (*accusing finger*.)

BOB. : Oh, oh ! It wasn't me ! I never thought !

DOB. : I did nothing, absolutely nothing !

CC. : (*with the air of a hanging judge*) You !

SS. : Of course it was ! They came running here from the inn, babbling like lunatics ! " He's come ! He's here ! " " He doesn't pay any money ! " Oh, yes ! They found a fine bird !

MAYOR : It would be them ! The town gossips ! " Tittle " and " Tattle." The devil fly away with the pair of you, and your Inspector-General !

SS. : The liars ! (*babel develops*.)

MAYOR : Running about throwing us into a panic ! Infernal chatterboxes !

JUDGE : Blackmailers !

CC. : Sheep in nightcaps !

POSTM. : Drunkards !

ANNA : Potbellied drivellers !

BOB. : Oh, please ! It wasn't me ! It was Peter Ivanovitch !

DOB. : No, Peter Ivanovitch ! You were certainly the first . . . !

BOB. : Really, Peter Ivanovitch you were the first ! Your stomach . . . (*these three speeches must not be lost in the tumult*.)

[*The doors fly open and in comes a tall, moustachio'd gendarme, dressed like a soldier, with crossed webbing, trousers, and busbee; he comes to attention.*]

GENDARME : His Excellency the Inspector-General appointed by Imperial decree has arrived from St. Petersburg. He is in residence at the hotel and requires your presence there, immediately.

Everybody is as if thunderstruck; the ladies utter simultaneous sounds of astonishment; the whole company remains petrified and transfixed in varied attitudes of wonder, horror, and stupefaction as

THE CURTAIN SLOWLY FALLS.